# My Business His Way

# My Business His Way:

## WISDOM & INSPIRATION FOR ENTREPRENEURS

### 2ND EDITION

## A'NDREA J. WILSON, PH.D.

Divine Garden Press

Published by Divine Garden Press
PO Box 371
Soperton, GA 30457

ISBN-13: 978-0615762425
ISBN-10: 0615762425

Cover Photo © Dennis Owusu-Anasah

Cover Design by A'ndrea J. Wilson

# Contents

# INTRODUCTION

Today, I drove past two businesses that had recently closed down. These were not small shops with four or five employees, but larger business that had been around for several years with multiple locations and more than two dozen employees. My jaw dropped in surprise and sympathy, relating to the unfortunate reality of business ownership. Even in the best economy, all businesses cannot thrive and some will eventually dissolve.

The truth that I had to accept was that business survival is not solely based on talent, intelligence, and a good idea. Many great people have come prior to me bearing all three of these traits and still have experienced failure. The difference between those who succeed and those who do not is the will of God. If God desires us to own a business, the world's financial status is irrelevant. But when we go out on our own, unconcerned with the Lord's agreement with our plans, we make ourselves susceptible to the heartache of disappointment.

In understanding how to own a business, I had to learn many things, but the most valuable lesson was how to surrender. I thought that creating my own enterprise would revolve around me and how I think business should be done. I was wrong. Starting and maintaining a successful business had nothing at all to do with me, but everything to do with God. I had to give up all of my perceptions, presumptions, and pretenses. If I was going to be a thriving leader in my community, God had to rid me of myself so that He could do a new thing in me. His will through my life was the objective. I had no idea of the monsoon that was headed in my direction.

The rains came and boy did it rain! A small trickle escalated into a heavy downpour, sending me running for cover. Just when I thought the wind and water would blow me away, the storm's intensity increased, knocking me off my feet and into a permanent praying position.

God brought the idea of writing this book when I was in the midst of the hardest moments of my journey. Not only did I find myself in the depths of struggle, but when I turned to my friends for support, they being just as ambitious as myself, were also in a sea of difficulties. Help seemed like a distant shore. But God was there, breaking me in order to rebuild me, His way. In the reconstruction phase, He placed in my heart a sense of compassion for business owners and the fight that occurs in our daily lives.

This book is written considering every emotion you will experience as an entrepreneur: joy, peace, sorrow, fear, faithfulness, appreciation, motivation, discouragement, and relief. It was created especially for you, to give you the hope, strength, and wisdom that are needed to survive in the business world. No matter what stage you are in, you can draw from the insight and encouragement that these devotions offer. If you are just starting out or pondering the vision God has given you, use this book to motivate you and teach you how your faith can be manifested into your endeavor from day one. If you already own a business, use this as a strengthening tool to increase your faith and keep you grounded.

# HOW TO USE THIS BOOK

Each devotional has four parts: the reading, scripture, lesson, and a prayer:

## READING

In your own time you can read the entire story from which the lesson is taken by referring back to the bible scriptures listed next to the reading header. This will help you get a clearer understanding of that lesson and the context from which it has been taken.

## SCRIPTURE

The devotion also contains an actual scripture from the bible for your convenience. The verses used are from the New International Version (NIV) and the New Century Version (NCV) as indicated, written in an easy to understand language. Reading the given scripture will guide you in your comprehension of the devotional lesson.

## LESSON

The scripture is broken down here for you in a way that applies to your business experiences. The lesson serves to encourage, uplift, develop, guide, and help you make better decisions related to your business and leadership activities. There are not fixed interpretations of the lessons. Allow the Lord to speak to you and give you meaning that is relevant to your situation.

## PRAYER

Use the prayer section to speak the Word of God over yourself and your business. Each prayer is directly associated with that lesson. You can come back to any of the prayers at any time when you feel the need to speak and mediate on these words.

I sincerely hope that as you read this book you will find the fresh air and energy that catapults you into business success. This book can be read once or over and over again. Let this book become a new source of support when no one around you can relate to what you are feeling or when the walls of failure are threatening to overtake you. Let it remind you that the Lord, your God is with you, and the battle is not yours, it's the Lord's.

## MY PRAYER FOR YOU

*Heavenly Father, thank You for leading this entrepreneur to this book. Speak to them through the scriptures, lessons, and prayers that this book contains. Reveal to them the greatness within themselves and how their passions line-up with Your will for their lives. As they meditate on these words, let it penetrate their hearts so that they will always know Your way of doing business. Allow them to make better decisions and to be a reflection of Your love, goodness, power, strength, and righteousness. You promised to make us the head and not the tail. You promised to make us the lender and not the borrower. You promised to give us wisdom, knowledge, protection, prosperity, joy, peace, and salvation if we would only have faith in You. I am believing with the soul who is reading this book, that You have great plans for their business, and as they devote time daily to understanding Your way of doing business, they will develop into the successful entrepreneur You created them to be. In the name of Jesus. Amen.*

# WILL I HAVE ENOUGH?

Reading: John 6:1-15

**When Jesus looked up and saw a great crowd coming toward him, he said to Phillip, "Where shall we buy bread for these people to eat?" He asked this only to test him, for he already had in mind what he was going to do. Phillip answered him, "Eight months' wages would not buy enough bread for each one to have a bite!" Another of his disciples, Andrew, Simon Peter's brother, spoke up, "Here is a boy with five small barley loaves and two small fish, but how far will they go among so many?"**

**John 6:5-9 (NIV)**

How many times do you as an entrepreneur struggle with the concept of will you have enough? Enough time, money, resources, help, energy, faith? You may have employees who depend on the success of you and your business to support their families and lifestyles. You may have customers who expect you to render certain products or services in an expected time frame or manner. On top of that, you have your own personal needs and desires to fulfill, and many times if seems as if there is just not enough. I imagine that is how the disciples felt when they looked at the multitude of people and compared it to the limited food resources provided by the boy with the bread and fish.

Jesus knew that he was preparing to perform a miracle, but He asked the disciples where they could get enough food to serve this great number of people. His asking was not out of ignorance to the food supply, but as a test. He wanted his followers to know that God was the real source of their supply. Naturally, the disciples started talking about how little food there was and how much it would cost. They failed their test and completely missed the point of Jesus' question. God is so much bigger than our limited physical supply and our financial resources. Jesus wanted the people to know that even when what we possess is not enough, God can always provide the increase that allows us to have more than enough.

Do you believe that God can give you and your business the increase needed? Do you trust Him to make-up for the things that you lack? Sometimes God allows for a shortage, just so that He can be glorified when He steps in and creates the miracle that takes us from a place of lack to a place of overflow. He desires that we rely completely on Him and not what we see. That is the definition of faith.

## PRAYER

*Lord, I know that I have not always trusted You to supply my needs and the needs of my business. At times, I lack faith and get caught up in what I see, forgetting who You are and what is possible through You. Forgive me for carnal thinking and help me to be a leader who is spiritually minded. There are resources and finances that my business requires, and I am in faith looking to You to provide. I believe that You are able to give me surplus so that I can fulfill the vision that You gave me. I thank You in advance for provision, and I asked that You be glorified as You bless me with this miracle. In Jesus' Name, I pray. Amen.*

# FAVOR & PROTECTION

Reading: 1 Samuel 18:1-30

**As they danced, they sang: "Saul has slain his thousands, and David has his tens of thousands." Saul was very angry; this refrain galled him. "They have credited David with tens of thousands," he thought, "but me with only thousands. What more can he get but the kingdom?" And from that time on Saul kept a jealous eye on David. The next day an evil spirit from God came forcefully upon Saul. He was prophesying in his house, while David was playing the harp, as he usually did. Saul had a spear in his hand and he hurled it, saying to himself, "I'll pin David to the wall." But David eluded him twice.**
**1 Samuel 18:7-12 (NIV)**

David was anointed by God to be the next King of Israel; Saul was no longer worthy of the position. While David was developing into his calling, Saul was becoming jealous and intimidated by David. The favor and protection of the Lord rested upon David and everything he did was a success. Even when Saul plotted evil against David, his plans blew-up in his face. David's anointing was so strong that all of the people loved him and celebrated his achievements.

In the same way, God calls us to fulfill a certain destiny. David's was to be the next king, but yours may be to own the next Fortune 500 Company or to create the next innovative product. Whatever you are anointed to do, you must be obedient to that calling. When you obey God, you are automatically shielded by His arms of protection and given favor similar to that of David. This does not mean that the enemy or people will not attack you. Conversely, this guarantees that they will. Out of jealousy and fear, others will come against you. God may even send hard times or difficulties your way as He sent an evil spirit to Saul that tried to harm David. The Lord's purpose is to strengthen and develop you while giving Him the opportunity to be glorified through your victory over the challenge. No matter if it's an attack from the enemy or a test from God, the Lord will still defend and uplift you.

When you are willing to trust God and move towards your destiny, success is inevitable. Not only will you be viewed as a conqueror to all those around you, but also those who dislike you and the very ones that tried to keep you from succeeding will have to acknowledge God's presence in your life. No matter who or what attempts to stand in your way, rest in the assurance that God has called you and destined you for greatness; no weapon formed against you will prosper (Isaiah 54:17).

## PRAYER

*Heavenly Father, I thank You for the calling you have placed on my life. You have destined me for greatness and I humbly accept Your call. I know there may be times when the enemy will try to destroy my dreams. I understand that there may be times when You allow struggles to come my way. But I also believe that if I am obedient to the mission You have spoken to me, that you will direct me, protect me, and elevate me. Make clear the anointing You have given me and how I can walk in it as I move forward as an entrepreneur. And as I achieve success, I will not forget to let my life glorify You, my King. In Jesus' Name. Amen.*

# THE TIME TO LEAD

Reading: 1 Chronicles 10:1-11:9

**All Israel came together to David at Hebron and said, "We are your own flesh and blood. In the past, even while Saul was king, you were the one who led Israel in their military campaigns. And the Lord your God said to you, 'You will shepherd my people Israel, and you will become their ruler.' " ...David had said, "Whoever leads the attack on the Jebusites will become commander-in-chief." Joab son of Zeruiah went up first, and so he received the command. David then took up residence in the fortress, and so it was called the City of David. He built up the city around it, from the supporting terraces to the surrounding wall, while Joab restored the rest of the city.**
**1 Chronicles 11:1-2, 6-9 (NIV)**

David was selected by God to become the next king when he was still a child. For many years he had to wait patiently while Saul held the position that he was promised. I believe at times it was hard for him to watch someone else whom wasn't worthy of the job get to rule as king when he knew that it was his destiny. Finally, Saul died and the kingdom is given to David. The people, knowing that David was next in line for the throne, welcomed him into his new position. David's first order of business after being sworn in was to reclaim Jerusalem and rebuild the city.

The bible tells us that there is a time for everything (Ecclesiastes 3:1). There is a time to wait, but there is also a time to take your place and carry out your purpose. When the opportunity arises for you to move forward with that dream or vision God has placed in you, what will you do? Will you allow fear, other obligations, or insecurities to keep you from stepping into position? Or, will you (like David) accept that it is your time and assume your new duties?

For many reasons, we often talk about our talents and gifts, but fail to activate them when the opportunity presents itself. We like the idea of becoming an entrepreneur, but we allow every excuse to stand between our blessing and us. We have to seize the moment when it comes. If David had not taken the job when it opened up, someone else eventually would have claimed it and he would have been waiting many more years before a 2nd chance would come again. Had he hesitated, he possibly would have never received another opportunity to be king. One of the biggest differences between those who are successful and those who are not is one's willingness to take action at the right time.

I like how David not only accepts his new title, but he also begins work immediately by making some necessary changes. Saul had not been leading with God's help so things were out-of-order. David had to do some cleaning-up to get the kingdom back on track. As leaders, some of our first responsibilities may be to fix another's mess or to problem-solve. We might have to come into an industry or field making serious changes and adjustments. Just like the Jebusites, not everyone will be happy about the new way of doing things, but if God is leading you, He will direct you in how to make these adjustments appropriately.

Finally, when you are called and it is your time, many people will not be surprised about your new success. In David's case, they came to him and reminded him that the Lord had called him to rule a long time ago. When you step into place as an entrepreneur, inventor, CEO, president, owner, or director you will find others saying to you, "I knew this would happen to you. You deserve this. God has anointed you. You were always a leader. Remember, remember?" A true leader leads long before they receive a title. A spirit-led entrepreneur knows when the time has come to transition from vision to reality.

## PRAYER

*Oh faithful God, You may have shown me the vision or given me the dream a while back, but I know that there is an appointed time for me to take my place in destiny. Help me to be sensitive to Your voice so that I don't miss my opportunity. Prepare me so that when the time comes, I am ready to take action immediately. Bring people into my life that can encourage me, support me, and confirm my vision. And when the time comes for me to live my dreams, let me know where to start and what to do. Give me divine wisdom and guide me to the areas that may need mending and renovating. Show me how to proceed despite the opinions and opposition of others. I trust that as long as You are by my side, I will, like David, become more capable of completing my God-given assignment. In Jesus' Name. Amen.*

# HEAR, LISTEN, AND UNDERSTAND

Reading: Matthew 13:1-23

**"The one who received the seed that fell among the thorns is the man who hears the word, but worries of this life and the deceitfulness of wealth choke it, making it unfruitful. But the one who received the seed that fell on good soil is the man who hears the word and understands it. He produces a crop yielding a hundred, sixty or thirty times what was sown."**
**Matthew 13:22-23 (NIV)**

Success and prosperity in your business is directly linked to your ability to hear, listen, and understand. In this parable, Jesus discusses the word being given to various types of listeners. Three of the types do not possess the ability to receive the word in a way that will cause fruitfulness. However, the last one, the man that is considered "good soil," is able to hear the word, understand it, and harvest it.

As entrepreneurs, we must strive to be good soil. Just as a good employee is someone who can hear a directive given by a superior, understand it, then act in accordance with the assignment, we also must take this approach. As an employee, one is subject to the instruction of their management. A good worker is someone who understands their job and can effectively complete their duties. As business owners, we do not have an earthly supervisor, but we do have a heavenly director. It is our responsibility to receive the word of God that He is speaking into our lives, understand it, and cultivate it until it produces an abundance of wealth and resources.

There will be times when God does not say anything at all to us. In those moments, it is our job to be still and continue to seek Him for direction. There are other times when the Lord gives us a word that may sound like a parable; it may be confusing, incomplete, or loaded with a lot of information that doesn't make sense. In those situations, we are to seek Him for wisdom and understanding, which He promises to freely give. We are also to move forward on the aspects of the word that we do comprehend as we wait for further instruction. Most often, we will find ourselves in one of these two positions, either not having a word at all or having an incomplete word. God knows that sometimes we are not ready for the full vision and that by not telling us everything at once, we are forced to seek and rely upon Him. However, there are times when the Lord paints the clearest, most complete vision or direction for us. When He does, He expects us to nurture that word in us and develop mental, physical, and spiritual evidence of our understanding.

Just because you work for yourself does not mean that you are not subject to the guidance of another. God becomes our leader as we pursue career freedom. Be sure to listen to the advice of God and avoid becoming thorny, rocky, or path places. Establish yourself as "good soil" that the Lord can sow good seed into.

## PRAYER

*Father, I may not have a manager or supervisor anymore, but I look to You as my guide and advisor. I know that You would never lead me down the wrong path and that I can have total confidence in Your counsel. Help me to be "good soil" that You can plant Your seeds of success into. Speak clearly to me. Give me understanding of Your word and how I should apply it in my life. Show me how to develop the vision You've given me. Allow my efforts to be fruitful and generate abundance that I can share with others. Let me be an example of what faith and obedience produces. In Jesus' Name. Amen.*

# STICKS & STONES

Reading: Acts 7

**At this they covered their ears and, yelling at the top of their voices, they all rushed him, dragged him out of the city and began to stone him. Meanwhile, the witnesses laid their clothes at the feet of a young man named Saul. While they were stoning him, Stephen prayed, "Lord Jesus, receive my spirit." Then he fell on his knees and cried out, "Lord, do not hold this sin against them." When he had said this, he fell asleep.**
**Acts 7:57-60 (NIV)**

Stephen was chosen by the disciples to be one of seven men that would care for the widows. He was a godly man who was plotted against because he intimidated those who opposed him. Stephen was willing to stand in faith and speak the truth to his accusers, which ultimately led to his death. Nevertheless, two things are interesting about his death. The first is that he prayed to God while he was being stone to forgive the very people who were taking his life. The second is that a man named Saul was there, witnessing and giving the stamp of approval on his death. Saul would soon have a name change and become Paul, the writer of many New Testament books and one of the most remembered followers of Christ.

This passage teaches us the importance of forgiveness. In your endeavors to grow your business, you will run into "haters" or people who oppose you. You will be talked about, laughed at, mocked, disliked, plotted against, and criticized. People will try to destroy you and everything you stand for. No matter what comes against you, forgive. Forgiveness is hard when people are evil towards you for no reason at all. When you are good to people and they still seek to harm you, it is hurtful and painful. Sometimes people you don't even know will attempt to come against your good name and the vision you are trying to fulfill. At these times, trust in the Lord that He will protect you and see you through to the end of the calling He has placed on your life.

Trusting God is only the first step. You must also forgive those who sin against you. When you do not forgive, the enemy wins because now your heart contains bitterness and resentment. You begin to carry that pain with you. It is harder to trust people and more difficult to have joy and peace. Your decisions are swayed by the wrong done against you. The way you view the world is altered and pessimism begins to creep into your being. How can God use you the way He desires if you are being pulled down by so much negative weight? How can your business flourish when things that are dead are consuming you? How can you reflect a godly attitude when dealing with employees and business associates when you are harboring mistrust in your heart? If you desire to blessed, fully and completely, you have to forgive and let go. That does not mean to submit yourself to being hurt again; it simply means to free yourself of those negative emotions and not allow them to dictate you future.

In addition, we must understand that not everything we go through is all about us. Sometimes, some things that we experience are for the benefit of others. In this situation, God was setting the stage to change the heart of Saul (Paul). Stephen's stoning is the first time Paul is mentioned in the Bible, meaning that before the incident, Paul was irrelevant to the mission of Christ, but soon afterwards, he became pivotal.

As you go through various trials, know that God has purpose for each one of them. Some are to test you, some to develop you, some to correct you, and some to bless others. Understand it is not always about you, but it is always about Him. As a leader who follows God, He will be glorified not only through your business success, but also through your ability to be used as a vessel to help others.

# PRAYER

*My God, thank you for the business You have given me and all the successes that comes with it. I trust that no matter who or what tries to oppose me, You will deliver me from it and elevate me higher. Help me to forgive those who try to destroy me. Comfort my broken heart and mend up my wounds. For those that I struggle to forgive, give me more love so that I can forgive them and let it go. I welcome You to use me as you please. I thank You that my experiences can bless others. Help me to remember that all of this is about You and for You. I surrender my life and business to You. I cry out "Yes Lord." In Your Son Jesus' name. Amen.*

# THE PEDESTAL

Reading: Philippians 2:1-11

**Your attitude should be the same as that of Christ Jesus: Who being in very nature of God, did not consider equality with God something to be grasped, but made himself nothing, taking the very nature of a servant, being made in human likeness. And being found in appearance as a man, he humbled himself and became obedient to death- even death on a cross! Therefore God exalted him to the highest place and gave him the name that is above every name, that at the name of Jesus every knee should bow, in heaven and on earth and under the earth, and every tongue confess that Jesus Christ is Lord, to the glory of God the Father.**
**Philippians 2:5-1 (NIV)**

Humility is a trait that most leaders today do not possess. People who are at the top are daily reminded of their success by the materialistic things around them and the praises they receive from their peers, family, friends, and fans. This constant exaltation leads to an inflated self-esteem, arrogance, and narcissism. The world has a tendency to elevate people based on their talents, prestige, and wealth. Contrary to its allure, the world's promotion is many times short-lived and usually produces vanity and self-deceit. Society tells you that you are someone special until someone who is more special comes along. When this occurs, you return to "nobody-ness" or you choose to stress yourself out in attempts to maintain the top position. That is not the way God intended us to live.

In the scripture, Paul is writing to the people of Philippi, encouraging them and giving them words of wisdom. In his writing, he tells them to remain humble. He explains that Jesus was humble and that they should strive to be like Him. Jesus knew who He was. He was the Son of God and had all of the rights and privileges to the Kingdom of Heaven. He could have come down to earth in a golden chariot, lived in a mansion, and put to death all those that opposed Him. He could have refused to die on the cross, separated Himself from the poor and sick, and adorned Himself with the finest robes and jewels. He was the Son of God; why not?

How many of us, because we are the son or daughter of someone important, think we should have the very best of everything? How many of us, because we own a certain successful business or are the leadership of a certain company, think that we are "all that?" How many of us have to have the flashiest car, the largest house, and the most expensive jewelry? Do all these things really make us important or even better than the next man? There is nothing wrong with having nice things, but most times our motives behind why we purchase nice things are wrong. If we adorn ourselves with materialistic things to look important, impress others, or flaunt our success, we are not living in the right spirit or mindset. Showing off is "selfish ambition and vain conceit."

Jesus had every right to parade his title, but He chose to be humble instead. Because he made himself a regular man and subjected Himself to death at the cross, God elevated him to the highest position in the kingdom. That at the name of Jesus every person must bow down and give him respect and honor.

As a business owner, you have a right to esteem yourself above your employees and others, but you can choose to remain humble. If you maintain a spirit of meekness, and care for the needs of your employees, consumers, and community, God will lift you up. God does not put us on a pedestal like the world does. When God raises you up, your increase can last a lifetime, not just a moment. When God blesses, you don't have to fret over keeping yourself in a certain position.

As long as you continue to abide in Him, He will take care of you.

## PRAYER

*Jesus, You are the perfect example of humility. I admit that I have at times boasted myself and vainly displayed your blessings in attempts to impress others and make myself feel important. I ask for Your forgiveness. I know that with You in my life, I am important, even if no one ever acknowledges who I am. As I move towards becoming a better leader, help me remain humble. It is You who are the sole source of my success, and I give the glory to You for all that I have and all that is coming my way. I will no longer attempt to elevate myself, but I will allow You to raise me up and make me the person You desire me to be. In the Name of Jesus, who I confess to be Lord. Amen.*

# "WHAT ARE YOU WAITING FOR?"

Reading: Joshua 18

**So Joshua said to the Israelites: "How long will you wait before you begin to take possession of the land that the Lord, the God of your fathers, has given you? Appoint three men from each tribe. I will send them out to make a survey of the land and to write up a description of it, according to the inheritance of each. Then they will return to me. You are to divide the land into seven parts..."**
**Joshua 18:3-5 (NIV)**

Moses led the children of Israel out of Egypt, but because of their lack of faith they were unable to immediately move into the promise land that God had intend for them. Moses passed the torch of leadership to Joshua, who led the Israelites into victory, conquering the cities and people who were residing in their promised land. Joshua gave this speech because although several tribes had claimed their inherited land, seven tribes had not.

As a leader there will be times when the people who are working for you or with you will not move and do the things they should be doing. There may be opportunities, assignments, projects, benefits, or duties that they could be handling or taking advantage of which they are not. Sometimes people are afraid and look to leadership to make the first move. Other times it is laziness, ignorance, complacency, or a lack of understanding. Regardless of the reason, it will be your responsibility to inform them of their unproductive ways and provide them with direction.

Joshua asked the question, "What are you waiting for?" God has clearly blessed them, others have taken their share of the land, but these last seven are just hanging out and being stagnant. There are always two types of workers: Group A and Group B. Group A requires very little supervision, motivation, and direction. They will take on tasks many times without being asked. They know their job well and can be depended on to handle business quickly, efficiently, and effectively. On the other hand, Group B requires a lot of supervision and direction. They need to constantly be motivated through pep talks and feedback. They will do a good job, but it will not be done as efficiently as Group A.

Joshua was dealing with Group B people. As a good leader he gave them the necessary pep talk. He then goes a step further and explains to them in detail what he expects them to do. He knows that if he doesn't communicate clearly and supervise them, the job may not get done right. As you gain employees or other workers you will find yourself working with both Group A and B types of people. Group B people are not bad employees they just need a lot more guidance from you. When dealing with people, figure out what group each can be classified into. According to their need for guidance, expect to give more or less direction to each individual. You will reduce stress and frustration by accepting that a worker falls into a certain group and that you must deal with them at their own level. In dealing with Group B people, don't be afraid to ask, "What are you waiting for?" if they fail to progress appropriately. You may have to specifically tell them step-by-step what is to be done and then monitor their development. Use your management skills to help them advance. But just like Joshua, direct them with love and respect.

## PRAYER

*Father God, thank You for placing me in a position of leadership. I am so grateful that You have brought people into my life to assist me in the vision You've given me. Thank You for the people you've brought me who are self-starters and can complete their tasks without me micromanaging them. I also thank You for the people who need my ore of my help. This offers me the opportunity to use the leadership and management talents and gifts that you put inside me. Help me to be patient, respectful, and full of love when dealing with workers that need my guidance. I trust You to provide me with the right people who can bring this vision to past. In Jesus' name. Amen.*

# WEALTH OR WISDOM?

Reading: 2 Chronicles 1

**God said to Solomon, "Since this is your heart's desire and you have not asked wealth, riches or honor, nor the death of your enemies, and since you have not asked for a long life, but for wisdom and knowledge to govern my people over whom I have made you king, therefore wisdom and knowledge will be given you. And I will also give you wealth, riches and honor, such as no king who was before you ever had and none after you will have."**
**2 Chronicles 1:11-12 (NIV)**

If God came to you right now and said to you, "Tell me what you want and whatever it is I will give it to you," what would you ask for? Many of us would ask for money, fame, possessions, a long life, and other things along this line. Some would even ask to be free of problems or to get rid of their enemies. Be honest with yourself, what would you ask for?

Solomon surpassed the temptation to ask for physical, materialistic, selfish, and things that would make his life more comfortable, and asked for wisdom and knowledge. This request proved to God that Solomon was not only the right man for the job, but also had a desire to be the best king he could be. Solomon understood that accepting this new role would not be easy. He had watched his father David struggle with making decisions that would impact numerous families. He was aware of all of the responsibilities that came with the title and recognized that being king was more than just glamour and glitz.

How many people desire to own their own business, but are physically, mentally, emotionally, and spiritually unprepared to do so? How many companies are founded by people who want all the glory, but don't want to do any of the work? How many times have you met leaders who are more concerned with making money and buying things than the development and growth of themselves and their subordinates? No matter what a company appears to be from the outside, a successful business is the byproduct of the wisdom, knowledge, development, and hard work of its leadership and employees.

Solomon had the right idea. He knew that if he was a good steward over the title God had given him, everything else would work out naturally. God not only gave Solomon the wisdom and knowledge he requested, but also rewarded him with more wealth, riches, and honor than any king had ever had in the past. God took it a step forward and also gave him more wealth, riches, and honor than any king would ever have in the future! That means that to this day and forevermore, no leader will ever have more wealth, riches, and honor than King Solomon had! This is the epitome of blessings and favor.

If you want your business to be highly blessed and favored, you must seek God for wisdom and knowledge. Before you ask Him for the prosperity, property, and power, you first need to ask Him for His presence and perception. You need understanding and judiciousness to make the right decisions at the right times. Solomon dedicates multiple chapters in the book of Proverbs to discussing the importance of having wisdom, and actually the entire book is assembled to provide wisdom and advice on various matters. God promises us that if we ask for wisdom, He will give it to us freely. Try it today and see how faithful He really is.

## PRAYER

*God Almighty, thank You for making me a leader and putting me in this position of leadership. To be a good steward over this business You've given me, I need to be endowed with wisdom and knowledge from You. I want to be like Solomon who was known for being a man of great wisdom. Yes, I need the finances and the resources, but I know if You first give me insight and understanding, all other blessings will flow. I trust You to lead and guide me daily in my mission to serve others as I serve You. Open my eyes, Lord; let me see and comprehend all that is laid out before me and help me to make the right choices. I will acknowledge You in all my ways and I believe that You will direct my paths. In Jesus' name. Amen.*

# WORD IS BOND

Reading: Numbers 32 & Joshua 22

**Then Joshua summoned the Reubenites, the Gadites, and the half tribe of Manasseh and said to them, "You have done all that Moses the servant of the Lord commanded, and you have obeyed me in everything I commanded. For a long time now-to this very day-you have not deserted your brothers but have carried out the mission the Lord your God gave you. Now that the Lord your God has given your brothers rest as he promised, return to your homes on the land that Moses the servant of the Lord gave you on the other side of the Jordan."**
**Joshua 22:1-4 (NIV)**

The Israelites were promised to inherit the land of Canaan, however, the tribes of Reuben, Gad, and Manasseh decided that they did not want to cross over the Jordan River because the land east of the Jordan was most suitable for their livestock. They made a promise to God and Moses, if they were given the land east of the Jordan that they would assist the rest of the Israelites in conquering and obtaining their inherited land. They agreed not to return home until every tribe had received their portion of the inheritance.

Even after the land has been conquered, these three tribes did not leave. They continued to wait until all the tribes settled on which land would belong to whom. Finally, after all the land had been handed out and every tribe had received what was due to them, Joshua gave Reuben, Gad, and Manasseh his blessing to go home. This is a prime example of keeping one's word. This is also a lesson in not abandoning others once you've received your blessing.

These three tribes made a promise and they kept it. It was a long time from the day they left their new homeland to the day they were able to go back. This is like purchasing a brand new home then immediately afterwards, being deployed by the military to a war that will last a few years. I am not sure of the length of time that they were away from their new homeland, but it definitely was not an overnight or weekend trip. Regardless of the duration, they remained faithful.

How quickly do you back out of promises? Are you someone known to follow through? Would you keep a promise over weeks, months, or years, even if it did not benefit you? Many of us do not have the patience and tenacity that these tribes possessed. Because they kept their word, they were eventually able to return home and acquire the land that was best for their people. Keeping our word not only betters our reputation, but it also puts us in position to be blessed by God because of our faithfulness.

In addition, this passage places emphasis on the commitment to others and their dreams. Many people are only concerned about "getting theirs" or achieving their own goals. When they reach their dreams they abandon ship, leaving others to fend for themselves, even though those abandoned were there for them and partially responsible for them achieving their objectives. This type of behavior is selfish, displays a lack of integrity, and leads to burned bridges and unfavorable karma.

Your word is everything, as an entrepreneur. You will make promises to employees, consumers, partners, vendors, relatives, friends, and God. Your aim should be to make promises that you intend to keep and to not to take commitments lightly. If a promise must be broken, it is your responsibility to apologize and explain to the person why you cannot follow through, then ask for forgiveness from them and God. You should also help those who have helped you, never forgetting who was there when you needed a helping hand. Once you are blessed and find yourself in a position of

success, give back to others and become active in the
fulfillment of their dreams.

## PRAYER

*Savior, help me to be an entrepreneur full of integrity. Allow people
to recognize me as someone who can be trusted and depended upon.
As I move towards my dreams, bring people into my life that can
help me get there. Once I reach my goals, remind me to help those
same people reach their dreams. Let me not be selfish, but I desire to
be a leader who gives back to my community, to my nation, and to
the world. Help me to keep the promises that I make. If I break a
promise, show me how to take responsibility and with humility and
seek forgiveness from the person whose promise has been broken. I
realize the importance of faithfulness because if it was not for Your
faithfulness to me, Heavenly Father, I would be lost and without
hope. Thank You for always being faithful to the promises You have
given me. In the name of Jesus. Amen.*

# IRREPLACEABLE

Reading: 1 Corinthians 12

**The eye cannot say to the hand, "I don't need you!" And the hand cannot say to the feet, "I don't need you!" On the contrary, those parts of the body that seem to be weaker are indispensable, and the parts that we think are less honorable we treat with special honor. And the parts that are unpresentable are treated with special modesty, while our presentable parts need no special treatment. But God has combined the members of the body and has given great honor to the parts that lacked it, so that there should be no division in the body, but that its parts should have equal concern for each other. If one part suffers, every part suffers with it; if one part is honored, every part rejoices with it.**
**1 Corinthians 12:21-26 (NIV)**

In this passage, Paul communicates the parallel between the physical body and the body of Christ, which is the church. His point is that although various body parts have different roles, they are all necessary to make the body function properly. The same point is made about the body of Christ; that although different people have different spiritual gifts, talents and titles, all are important in operating the church.

The same message can be reflected in your business. Depending on the size of your company, you will have a number of people working for you to accomplish a certain goal. You will also have other venders, partners, collaborators, etc. who do not work for you, but still are important because they are working with you to achieve their own goals, as well as yours. Regardless of how many people you network with or employ, and despite their title or role, all are essential to the success of your business.

Companies that have high turnover rates are typically in violation of the golden rule. They lose employees because they treat people based on their level of prestige in the company. Managers and supervisors are given better benefits and greater appreciation than field workers and office staff. Soon, the lower level employees, feeling overstressed, overworked, and underpaid, begin to complain about and resent their leaders. The result: high turnover and low production, equaling reduced profits.

If we take wisdom from these verses, we understand that no matter the role of an individual, each person directly influences our success. A company should be looked at as a family or a body. All members are essential to the proper functioning and the profitability of the business. When we view our employees in this fashion, we learn to take better care of and appreciate all of them. Workers who are respected, valued, and esteemed become loyal employees who are happy, fulfilled, and more effective.

Think back to when you were under the leadership of another. When you were an employee, how were you treated? Did the way you were treated influence your devotion, satisfaction, and commitment to that company? Were you more or less productive dependent on the way you felt about upper management? Were you even willing to stay longer, work harder, and receive less pay when you worked for people who showed genuine care and concern for you? Most people would probably agree that better work conditions equate to employee stability.

Gaining this knowledge, what will you do differently today? Will you celebrate a receptionist's birthday? Will you provide bonuses after a record-breaking quarter? Will you say thank you to field workers at the end of a hard day? Will you send a sick employee a get-well card? Will you offer criticism with love and gentleness? Will you give someone a raise when it is deserved? There are so many ways that we can show our gratitude towards those who work for and with us. Start today by acknowledging every single person in your business as irreplaceable.

## PRAYER

*Holy One, I praise You for every gift and blessing You've given me. Every person I work with is a treasure from You. You loved me enough to not only give me a business, but also to send people my way that would believe in the vision You have given me. Help me to show my appreciation every day to the ones who make this dream possible. Remind me not to show favoritism to upper management, but to know that every individual from the secretary to the vice president is essential in the success of this business. Show me new ways that I can be a blessing to my staff. Let me be a leader who displays love, kindness, and sincerity. In the revered name of Jesus. Amen.*

# FREE TO SUCCEED

Reading: Acts 16

**About midnight Paul and Silas were praying and singing hymns to God, and the other prisoners were listening to them. Suddenly there was such a violent earthquake that the foundations of the prison were shaken. At once all the prison doors flew open, and everybody's chains came loose.**
**Acts 16:25-26 (NIV)**

**"So if the Son sets you free, you will be free indeed."**
**John 8:36 (NIV)**

A slave girl who told fortunes and was under the oppression of a spirit had been following Paul and Silas around, provoking them. Finally, Paul commanded the spirit out of her under the authority of Jesus. When the owners of the girl realized that they could no longer make money from the girl's predictions, they accused Paul and Silas of wrongdoing and had them put in jail. Instead of complaining, these disciples worshiped God, which resulted in their chains, as well as the chains of all the other prisoners, to be loosed. The story continues on to report the salvation of the prison guard and his family. In just a few verses, many people received freedom. The slave girl, Paul and Silas, the prisoners, the prison guard, and his family, all experienced some type of freedom in the sixteenth chapter of Acts.

We all have chains. We all have issues in which we need to be freed. Whether it is the need for salvation itself–being free from sin–or the breaking of a personal bondage in which we have struggled with even after our commitment to Christ, we all wear invisible chains. This repression occurs in our minds and affects every portion of our lives, including our businesses. Yes, that thing that burdens you affects your ability to be as successful as you should be, even if the problem is completely irrelevant to your company.

You may wonder how this is possible. How can my personal issues negatively affect my business? Whatever we struggle with individually will dictate who we are as a person and how we operate daily. We carry all of ourselves to our careers: the good, the bad, and the chains. Your leadership abilities are directly affected by whatever holds you down. As an entrepreneur, you are the foundation of your business and your company will reflect all that you are. If you really want to know what issues are holding a leader back, look at his or her business, employees, and professional environment. It will give you a good indication of their spirit.

Pray and ask God to free you from your chains so that you can be a better business owner. The word tells us that whom Jesus sets free is really and completely free. Your bondage could come in many forms: fear, abuse, low self-esteem, generational curses, weight and eating disorders, drugs and alcohol, sexual problems and addictions, anger, depression, perfectionism, unfaithfulness, dishonesty, jealousy, negativity, narcissism, selfishness, vanity, greed, etc. Honestly, assess yourself and identify the issues that hold you hostage from being your very best. The Son waits with open arms to give you the freedom you desire.

## PRAYER

*Jesus, I come to You truthfully, seeking the freedom that only You can give. You know the issues that have kept me bound and unable to serve You with all of my heart, mind, and body. I need You right now. Please remove oppression from my life. I especially pray for freedom over <u>(Fill in the blank)</u>. I believe that whom You set free is truly free indeed. Thank You for the loosing of chains that is occurring at this very moment. Let my newfound freedom be reflected in my life, attitude, and business. This I pray in the bondage-breaking name of Jesus. Amen*

# ALL A PART OF THE PLAN

Reading: Ephesians 1

**In him we were also chosen, having been predestined according to the plan of him who works out everything in conformity with the purpose of his will; in order that we, who were the first to hope in Christ, might be for the praise of his glory.**
**Ephesians 1:11-12 (NIV)**

Remember these words: we were also chosen, predestined according to the plan, conformity with the purpose of His will, and His glory. These two verses reveal an amazing truth to us: God has an ultimate plan and we are a part of it. Let's examine these words closer:

*We were also chosen.* To "be chosen" means that there were other options, but we were selected despite what other alternatives existed.

*Predestined according to the plan.* In advance, a plan was created that was certain to be fulfilled.

*Conformity with the purpose of His will.* Things will submit to or obey with the objectives of God's will.

*His glory.* The result is that He will be exalted.

In this passage, we learn that before time God created a plan: we were selected to follow the will and goal of God, which is for Him to be uplifted.

God's plan is in effect. We can either decide to be in line with His plan or not. He has already picked us and put us into His blueprint. The house will be built.

Every experience we have is intended to align us with the will of God. He molds us through triumph and heartache, pressing us to the point of surrender. He squeezes all the "me" out of us, leaving us with nothing left but "He." In the end, He is glorified and His will is fulfilled.

As business owners, we must be sure to stay within God's will. Our companies are blessed as we conform to His plan. It is our businesses, but He must be at the center of it. If God is not at the root of your endeavor, when the winds blow, and they will, it will fly away. Only what you do for Christ will last. This does not mean your business must be a religious organization, it simply means that your company should aim to give glory and honor to the Father. Submit your business to Him, comply with His will, and watch God create miracles every day for you.

## PRAYER

*God Most High, I submit this company to You. I desire for You to be at the heart of everything that this company does and is. Although I am in this position of leadership, all of this belongs to You. Thank You for choosing me and trusting me with stewardship over this great company. Help us to glorify You in our daily operations. Show us Your will and how we can stay aligned with it. We give You praise, Holy One, for all that we are and all that we shall be. In Jesus' name. Amen.*

# THE 13ᵀᴴ HOUR

Reading: John 11:1-44

**When he heard this, Jesus said, "This sickness will not end in death, No, it is for God's glory so that God's Son may be glorified through it." Jesus loved Martha and her sister and Lazarus. Yet when he heard that Lazarus was sick, he stayed where he was two more days.**

**John 11:4-6 (NIV)**

The story of Jesus raising Lazarus from the dead is one of the most popular miracles performed by Jesus in the Bible. Jesus receives word that Lazarus is sick, but instead of rushing to his side to save him, Jesus waits until He hears that Lazarus has died before He goes to visit him. Once He gets to where Lazarus and his family are, Lazarus has already been buried in a tomb for four days. Despite this fact, Jesus commands Lazarus back to life. This miracle leads to the Pharisees plotting to arrest and kill Jesus.

What is interesting about this story is that Jesus waits until all hope is lost before stepping in and rescuing His friend from death. Sometimes, this is what happens today in our lives and the lives of our businesses. We find ourselves in tough situations, struggling with debt or lack of resources, dealing with problem customers or employees, or facing complete failure. At a certain point, all hope is lost and it seems that even if Jesus comes, it will still be too late. This is called the 13th hour; when God comes to our aid after the fact, when the damage is already done.

Nevertheless, this was Jesus' intention. When He heard Lazarus was sick, He knew that Lazarus would die, but the death was not permanent. The plan was to allow Lazarus to die so that God and Jesus could be recognized. When we think we are experiencing the death of our business, it may not be a true death; it may be an opportunity for God to be glorified. God may be allowing things to become utterly out-of-control and so bad that there is absolutely nothing you can do to revive your company or the situation. At the moment when you throw your hands up in defeat and cry out, "I surrender this to you Lord because I've done all that I know how; only you can save me now;" that is when Jesus shows up and speaks to your circumstance saying, "Come out!"

God wants to use you and your business to get the praise He deserves. He may want to increase your faith, He may desire to prove Himself to others through your testimony, or He may even want to put you in a position where you have no choice but to give Him the credit. Regardless of His reason for delaying your breakthrough, it does not mean He's not going to come through for you. Like the popular saying goes, "God's delay is not God's denial." Expect the appearance of Jesus, even when the curtains have closed, the lights have been turned off, and the play seems to be over. When you least expect it God, the Lord of the Impossible, can show up and create a brand new beginning.

## PRAYER

*Lord, all praises belong to You. You are God all by Yourself and I honor You. Just as You raised Lazarus from the dead, You are able to restore my dead situation. I need You right now like never before. I have done everything I know how to make this business work. I've even cried out to You. But even now as I watch my circumstance lie here, seemingly dead, I know You are still able to speak life into it. I surrender it to You. Raise my business from its sleeping status. Breath into it, allow Your saving power to revive it. Do this so that You can be glorified. Give me a testimony that will bless and touch the lives of others. Increase my faith through this miracle. I thank You, my King, and give you the highest praise of hallelujah. In the name of Jesus. Amen.*

# OBEDIENCE 101: PART 1

Reading: Deuteronomy 28

**If you fully obey the Lord your God and carefully follow all his commands I give you today, the Lord your God will set you high above all the nations on earth...The Lord will grant that the enemies who rise up against you will be defeated before you. They will come at you from one direction but flee from you in seven. The Lord will send a blessing on your barns and on everything you put your hand to. The Lord your God will bless you in the land he is giving you.**
**Deuteronomy 28:1, 7-8 (NIV)**

If God has placed a vision inside you and has led you to fulfill His plan through entrepreneurship, it is vital that you be obedient. Not only does the success of your business depend on your willingness to submit to His will, but also your triumph and satisfaction as an individual are directly impacted by your obedience.

In Deuteronomy, we find Moses speaking to the children of Israel after freeing them from Egypt and giving them the Ten Commandments. He provides them with laws that they should follow if they desire to remain in the good graces of God. Then he tells them that if they are willing to obey the Lord, they will receive blessings in every aspect of their lives.

The same remains true for us. If we are willing to obey God and His words to us, we can also receive blessings in every area of our lives. God can give us protection, prestige, and prosperity. He can take us to the top and keep us there. He can bring us out of debt and make us the lender. There is so much God will do for us if we would only just obey.

God has a plan for you and your business. He delights in our success because He is glorified through us. Yet He cannot give us all that He has for us if we are not willing to take the message He has given us and apply it to our lives. We must submit ourselves to His will and direction. When we become eager to move outside of our own agendas and ourselves, and follow the vision He has given us, He then becomes enthusiastic about opening up the heavens for us.

If you desire to see your life and the lives of others around you blessed, obey. If you want to see your dreams come true, obey. If there are some changes God has been speaking to you about, obey. If the vision He has given you is so strong and clear, obey. Obedience leads to the blessings of the Lord. Tell fear, doubt, your enemies, and any other thing that comes against the word of God, "Today I will obey and today I will be blessed."

## PRAYER

*My Lord and Savior, I come before You as humbly as I know how. You are my God and I know that Your words to me are for my good. I may not understand Your thoughts or Your ways, but I submit to them. The vision You have given me is a direct order from You. In the past, I may have allowed other issues like fear and doubt to keep me from following Your directions and for this, I ask for forgiveness. From this day on, I commit to obeying You and Your commands to me. I desire the blessings that come with my obedience and I ask that you shower me with Your favor. Make me the head, bless everything I touch, give me success in all that I do, and destroy everything that comes against me. I surrender to You and I trust You with my hopes and dreams. In the name of Christ Jesus. Amen.*

# OBEDIENCE 101: PART 2

Reading: Deuteronomy 28

> **However, if you do not obey the Lord your God...The Lord will send on you curses, confusion and rebuke in everything you put your hand to, until you are destroyed and come to sudden ruin because of the evil you have done in forsaking him...You will be unsuccessful in everything you do; day after day you will be oppressed and robbed with no one to rescue you.**
>
> **Deuteronomy 28:15, 20, 29 (NIV)**

God promises to bless us when we are obedient, but there is a flipside to this pledge. If we do not obey, we then become cursed. Have you ever met someone that seems cursed? No matter what they do, it falls apart. They are never happy and everything they touch goes completely wrong. Even when they try to do well, they end up failing miserably. Do you know anyone like that? If you do, you probably would never want to trade shoes with them. That type of living is the worst and can only lead to frustration, anger, depression, and hopelessness.

When we disobey God, we risk becoming that cursed person. We risk not only the failure of our businesses, but also the complete deterioration of everything in our lives for which we have worked so hard. A few of the omitted verses from this passage speaks of planning to marry a woman and having her taken by another, building a house and not living in it, and planting a vineyard and not ever enjoying its fruits. Can you image the sorrow and pain of living this way?

God has given you a purpose, a plan, a vision that only you can fulfill. He has placed inside of you everything you need to accomplish it. Whatever you don't have, He will either give it to you or send someone into your life who has it. All you have to do is walk it in. Move forward and follow the instructions He has communicated to you. Do not let anything stand in your way; your blessings are dependent on your faith and follow-through.

No matter what, be determined to be obedient. Some of us are living with less than God has for us simply because we are not obeying. Some of us are struggling, hurting, sick, broke, failing, crying, dying, being robbed, and being oppressed daily because of our refusal to abide by the commands of the Lord. Choose blessings over curses by deciding that you will submit. Flee from disobedience and forsake not the Lord. Both blessings and curses await you. Which one can you live with?

## PRAYER

*Father God, thank You for the grace and mercy You have bestowed upon me. Thank You that even when I have not followed Your word, You have given me another chance. I should be destroyed, but Your love has blessed me despite what I deserve. From this moment on, I choose to obey You. I hear Your voice, and I see Your plan for my life. Help me to be faithful with Your directives. Free me from any curses that are on my life due to past disobedience. Restore my business and myself from this place of struggle. Break every single yoke and stronghold operating against me. Release all the blessings You have for me. I surrender to Your will. I claim in Jesus' name that my brighter days will begin today. Amen.*

# NO EXCEPTIONS

Reading Ecclesiastes 9:1-12

**I have seen something else under the sun: The race is not given to the swift or the battle to the strong, nor does food come to the wise or wealth to the brilliant or favor to the learned; but time and chance happen to them all.**

**Ecclesiastes 9:11 (NIV)**

This is one of the most misquoted verses in the bible. For many years, I actually thought that this verse said, "The race is not given to the swift nor to the strong, but the one that endures to the end." Why did I think this? Because I heard so many people quote it that way and I assumed it was written in this manner in the Bible. Several years ago, I found this verse and was amazed that it did not say anything about endurance or tenacity. It's not that perseverance isn't vital to winning the race, but it just is not the conclusion to this verse. This taught me to find truth and wisdom for myself and not rely on the facts and opinions brought to me by unreliable sources. The word advises us to "study to show thyself approved" (2 Timothy 2:15).

This verse teaches us that no matter how smart, strong, fast, or wise we are; we all will experience the issues of life and time. We all will grow old and face death. We all will experience love, hurt, joy, and pain. Everyday can't be sunny, but the storm does not last forever. No one is exempt from the flow of life. Even Jesus was subject to the difficulties of this world.

As a business owner, you and your company will experience the various seasons: autumn, winter, spring, and summer. Which season are you currently in? Is it autumn? Are you watching some of your hard work slowly fall apart? Is production slowing down? Are attitudes growing colder? Is the momentum dying; is the vision becoming less clear?

Are you in winter? Is everything at a stand-still? Does it seem like no matter what you do, progress is impossible? Have you lost almost everything you have built? Does your company feel dead and buried underneath debt and failure?

Is it spring? Are you sowing seeds of faith and resources? Do you feel hopeful at the sight of small advances? Are resources sprouting up in places you did not expect? Is the vision growing and becoming more and more in focus?

Or is it summer? Are you experiencing harvest? Are blessings overtaking you? Is there an overflow of resources? Has the vision been manifested into the physical?

Regardless of your current season, your business will experience all of them. Every company, even the most successful have at one time been in an autumn or winter season. They made it through those tough times because the leadership stayed devoted to the vision and did not allow hardships to steal their faith. When you find yourself drowning and your company dying, remember that there are no exceptions to the rule. Time and chance happen to us all. The word says that race is not given to the biggest and the best. However, it also tells us that we can do all things through Christ Jesus who gives us strength.

## PRAYER

*Most Holy One, You are God all by Yourself. I understand that I am not an exception to the rule and that time and chance will happen in my life and in the life of my business. No matter the current season of my business, I trust that You will lead me from my autumns and winters into my springs and summers. During the hard times, remind me that You are Lord and able to strengthen and keep me. My business will not die in winter, but it will survive to experience the miracle of spring and the favor of summer. Right now my Savior, give me the faith, perseverance, and wisdom to stay true to the vision You've given me, and to know that brighter days are ahead. In the name of Jesus. Amen.*

# START HERE

Reading: Mark 12:28-34

**"The most important one," answered Jesus, "is this: 'Hear, O Israel, the Lord our God, the Lord is one. Love the Lord your God with all your heart and with all your soul and with all your mind and with all your strength.' The second is this: 'Love your neighbor as yourself,' There is no commandment greater than these."**

**Mark 12:29-31 (NIV)**

The two greatest commandments: to love God with all your might and love others as much as you love yourself. If we could start here in our lives and our walks with God, so many of us would think and behave completely different than we currently do. In loving God first, then loving others, we find no room for selfishness or self-centeredness.

Many of us struggle in our relationship with God because we will not put Him first. We love Him, but not with everything in us. Because our love for Him is not complete, we find ourselves consumed with our own pleasures and desires. He asks us to follow Him, but we, like the man on the road in Luke 9:59, want to do our own thing first. If we truly loved God with our whole heart, soul, mind, and strength like He commands, we would find it amazingly easy to follow Him at all costs.

Selfishness also comes into place because we do not love others to the capacity that God instructs. We hurt, disappoint, deceive, mistreat, and do not appreciate others because we do not love them as we love ourselves. It is so simple to do others wrong when they pose a threat to us or are in our way because we love ourselves so much more. We tell ourselves, "I'm just doing what's best for me." But what if we did what was best for all of us? How differently would our choices be then?

As a leader, it is important that you set the example within your company of following these two most important commandments. When your subordinates witness you loving God and loving others, they will replicate your actions causing a domino effect of care, kindness, and community. How much more productive could your business be if each employee and manager loved each other and most importantly loved God? How would customers respond to your business if every time they reached out to you they felt loved, cherished, and respected? What would the environment feel like–going to work every day–if everyone at your office had gentleness, goodness, and grace in their spirits? This type of energy is possible if you as the leader display it first. Ask God to keep you faithful to these two commandments on a daily basis and expect the mood of your place of business to transform to one that overflows with love. If you desire to be a better leader, start here.

# PRAYER

*Messiah, from this day forward, I choose to live within Your commandments to me. I put You first and I give You all of me. I strive to love You with my whole heart, soul, mind, and strength. Give me more love so that I can love my brother just as much as I love myself. Help me not to be selfish or self-centered, but let love live at the root of all of my thoughts and actions. Let me be an example of love in my business and allow the love that I carry to spill out onto the hearts and minds of my subordinates. Create a wave of love that fills our work environment and flows out into the world. Thank You for the greatest gift You give which is love. In Jesus' name. Amen.*

# THE FIRST PEDICURE

Reading: John 13:1-16

**Jesus knew that the Father had put all things under his power, and that he had come from God and was returning to God; so he got up from the meal, took off his outer clothing, and wrapped a towel around his waist. After that, he poured water into a basin and began to wash his disciples' feet, drying them with the towel that was wrapped around him.**
**John 13:3-5 (NIV)**

Of all the things that Jesus did while He walked this earth, the washing of His disciples feet was probably one of the most unusual and powerful acts of leadership. Whenever I am getting a pedicure, I find myself fascinated by the people who serve others in this way, day after day. Their entire profession is centered on being at someone's feet. How humbling is that? How many of us could devote ourselves to serving others in this way?

Jesus washing the feet of His disciples provides us with an example of what a true leader is: someone who serves. This is opposite of what most of us have been taught. Many think that being a leader is about being at the top, directing people, telling others what to do, and having everyone serve you. Nevertheless, in these verses Jesus reveals to us that even the greatest leader was lowly enough to serve His followers.

It is easy to bark out orders constantly and to dominate the spotlight, but it is difficult to submit yourself to the lowest position: the floor. Washing feet requires that you position yourself as close as possible to the floor so that you can adequately tend to the person's feet. Lowering yourself through servant-hood when you have the title of the leader involves security, compassion, meekness, and appreciation, but results in loyalty, development, strength, and wisdom.

As an entrepreneur, you must understand that you cannot always be in the power position. You must being willing to follow and serve when it's appropriate. There will be people that God will send to you that have gifts and talents that deserve recognition and it will be your role to let them shine. You may turn important assignments over to an able or more experienced employee; you may give credit for a particular business advancement to an assistant, secretary, or manager. You may even ask for help or advice from a worker younger than yourself. Know when to lead and when to serve. A good leader understands this concept and is not too arrogant or self-absorbed to wash a subordinate's feet.

## PRAYER

*Almighty Father, I give all praise and honor to You for being the greatest leader and example of leadership to me. Through Your Son, You've taught me how to love, give, and serve. Help me never to become so proud that I cannot serve the very people who I expect to serve me. Teach me to know the difference between times when I should lead and times when I should follow. Surround me with wonderful people who I can esteem and recognize. Remind me that when one of my employees shines, that light reflects upon my entire company. Thank You, Christ for being the perfect example of what it is to have a spirit of humility. In the name of Jesus. Amen.*

# SOMETHING NEW

Reading: Jeremiah 18

**"Go down to the potter's house, and there I will give you my message."** So I went down to the potter's house, and saw him working at the wheel. But the pot he was shaping from the clay was marred in his hands; so the potter formed it into another pot, shaping it as seemed best to him.
**Jeremiah 18:2-4 (NIV)**

The potter takes what is damaged and makes something new out of it, something he feels is appropriate. There are two lessons that can be learned from this text: restoration and new purpose.

First, the fourth verse speaks of restorative power. The potter takes the disfigured clay and shapes it into something good, something right. That is what God is capable of doing with us as leaders. Because of sin and our past experiences, we are ruined, damaged, and marred. When God should just throw us away and start all over, he chooses to use us anyway and turn us into something new. At the beginning of your business venture, you will be a certain person with specific ideas, thoughts, plans, beliefs, attitudes, etc. However, if you allow God to develop you, a year or two into your endeavor you will notice that you are not the same person you used to be. God is molding and changing you into the leader you were destined to become. This process only works if we surrender to His shaping and trust being in His hands.

Second, the verse communicates a new purpose. The initial pot possibly used to be one that held water, but now it can be used for cooking. Maybe it was a pot for planting flowers and now it waters them. Whatever the former pot was used for, the old pot has been transformed into another, for the purpose the potter desires. As entrepreneurs, God will not only change us, but also recreate us into what He wants us to be. He knows what the best use for us is and if we would submit, He can create us into the leaders that will be more effective for kingdom goals. You may have been a teacher, lawyer, doctor, warehouse manager, cashier, counselor, cook, operator, or mechanic, but God can make you a business owner, CEO, board chair, director, president, founder, or partner. He does what seems best to Him.

When you feel yourself in the midst of a storm, God is shaping you. When money and other resources are low, God is forming you. When your prayers seem repetitious and unanswered, God is molding you. When discouragement and fear threaten to take over, God is making you. When no one understands what you are going through or the stress you feel, God is changing you. There is safety in the Potter's hands. Allow Him to make you better than you were before.

## PRAYER

*God, You are the Potter of my life and my business. You are the one who created me as well as this vision that I strive to bring to life. I submit myself to Your molding, shaping, and forming. You know the person that I need to be to fulfill the will You have for my life. The ruined and damaged person I used to be is no more. Change me from the old into something new. Most High, I place myself in the safety of Your hands for You to create in me what You feel is best. In the name of Jesus. Amen.*

# RETURN TO ME

Reading: Malachi 3

**I the Lord do not change. So you, O descendants of Jacob, are not destroyed. Ever since the time of your forefathers you have turned away from my decrees and have not kept them. Return to me, and I will return to you," says the Lord Almighty. "But you ask, 'How are we to return?' Will a man rob God? Yet you rob me. But you ask, 'How do we rob you?' In tithes and offerings."**

**Malachi 3:6-8 (NIV)**

Many of us do not like to hear or think about tithing and giving offerings. As a business owner, especially a new or small company, you are probably making little to no money. All of your funds may be tied up in paying bills and paying employees. You may be experiencing extreme financial lack and giving up any percentage of your revenue may seem foolish.

As an entrepreneur myself, I had to learn that tithing was not about giving my much needed money to some church, but about trusting God enough to give Him something that I didn't have to give. It is about putting Him first and acknowledging that He is the true source of my prosperity. For me, it came to the point that I needed to give tithes and offerings to Him because I was so desperate for financial change that I was afraid if I didn't step out in faith and give, everything I had worked so hard for would crumble.

It is not easy giving the first tenth of your earnings to anyone, even God. It takes a lot of faith to do so when you are using money that should be going towards a bill or when debt is overtaking you. When you finally get a few dollars in your hands, the last thing you may want to do is give to a church that is prospering and has a pastor that is driving a bigger and better car than you are.

In the process of starting my business, I experienced serious monetary drought. There were times when I did not have enough gas in my car to get to a potential client's house. There were times when I was on my last roll of toilet paper with less than four dollars in the bank and my credit cards were maxed out. I have experienced every bill being past due and utilities in my home being turned off. When I went to the kitchen to eat, I had one thing, but not the complimentary item so I couldn't eat such as, waffles, but no syrup or sandwich fillers, but no bread. I felt like a complete failure and wondered why God was taking so long to bring me out.

Despite my status, God put in my heart to give. He reminded me that He did not need my money and that He ultimately controlled whether or not my business and I survived. He explained to me that He needed to know that I really trusted Him and wanted to make sure I was ready to handle the increase that He had for me. Therefore, with a hopeful spirit I gave, praying He would catch my fall. Soon it became somewhat of a game. I would give to see how quickly and miraculously He could give me it back with heavenly interest. I would take the increase and give again, watching and waiting.

Waiting on God is one of the hardest lessons I have ever learned. Nevertheless, God is faithful and I never hit the ground. He caught me. I returned to Him and He returned to me. If you desire to be taken care of even at the most difficult times of this business endeavor, God is whispering, "Return to me." Think about it like this: If He is God, what do you really have to lose?

## PRAYER

*Jehovah, You are the God who provides. Starting and maintaining a business is not easy and extremely uncomfortable. I need Your provision and financial assistance. If You don't bless me with customers, products, and monetary resources, my business will fail and I will be left without. I return to You and offer my first fruits to you. I trust You with what I don't have. You know my struggle and lack, and I expect You to be true to Your word and return to me. Rebuke the devourer and open the windows of heaven, pouring me out blessings that I do not have room to contain. Catch my fall right now; don't allow me to hit the ground. You are the only one who can save me and give me the financial freedom I crave. Thank You, Lord, for the increase You are right now manifesting into the physical for me. In Jesus' name. Amen.*

# USE WHAT YOU GOT

Reading: 2 Kings 4

**Elisha replied to her, "How can I help you? Tell me, what do you have in your house?" "Your servant has nothing there at all," she said, "except a little oil."**
**2 Kings 4:2 (NIV)**

The woman in this story was a widow who was worried that her creditors would take her sons away as slaves because she could not pay her debts. How often do we feel as she did, that the very things we love, that what we have worked so hard to birth and develop will be snatched away from us because we do not have enough money? Phone calls and letters from bill collectors, notices threatening to cut off services, ruin your credit, repossess items, or sue you may be a very real part of your life. This is where the widow is; overwhelmed by the burden of her debt.

She brings her problem to the man of God and he asks her what does she have? Her answer is, "Nothing, but a little oil." He then instructs her to borrow as many jars as she can get her hands on, get alone with God and her family, and use what she has to get what she wants. She obeys Elisha and in front of her very eyes, a miracle is performed. Her little oil is transformed into much oil and she is able to turn a profit with it, paying her debts as well as living off the access.

We are all at risk of being overtaken by our financial obligations. Especially as entrepreneurs, we put ourselves in debt's path in a faithful attempt to gain career fulfillment and freedom. If you feel like the widow, today God is asking you, what do you have? What is left? What skills, talents, resources, people, and items are accessible to you? God never leaves us with nothing at all; He always allows us to have at least one or two things that He can use to bless us. Once you identify what you have, God then is able to create overflow in your life through that thing.

Now before you get too excited, let me make an important point. You need to identify what God wants to use to bless you however; there may be catch to it. Sometimes that thing is what your business offers, sometimes it is not. Just because God has given you a business does not mean that your biggest blessings will come from it. Some of us are like the parable of the talents. We may have more than one gift or "thing" God wants to use. Your business may not be utilizing that "thing" God desires to use to create your miracle. The vision for your company may be from God, but the blessing you need might come from a different direction. My business was interior design, but my "thing" is writing. My biggest blessings were always associated with the gift of writing.

One last thought. You may be afraid to use the money you have because you feel it is not enough and you fear that if you use the little you have, you will end up with nothing. That kind of thinking is unproductive and faithless. Jesus would probably say to you, "O ye of little faith." Pray and ask God how to use the little resources He has given you to obtain great and overflowing blessings in your life and business.

## PRAYER

*Most High God, thank You for never leaving me completely empty and without. Even in the driest times, You provide me with at least one "thing" that you can use to bless me. Reveal to me where the true blessings of my life reside. Show me where I have little that can be transformed into much. If I am using the wrong thing or overlooking a gift or resource, reveal it to me and instruct me on how to use it effectively. Let me be a person of great faith who is not afraid to take little things and trust You to create miracles with them. Guide me as I sacrifice comfort for the bigger things You have for me. Allow my blessings to flow continually like the widow's oil. Thank You, Almighty. In the name of Jesus. Amen.*

# THE LONELY BATTLE

Reading: Matthew 26:31-55

Then he returned to his disciples and found them
sleeping. "Could you men not keep watch with me for
one hour?" he asked Peter. "Watch and pray so that
you will not fall into temptation. The spirit is willing,
but the flesh is weak."...When he came back, he again
found them sleeping, because their eyes were heavy.
So he left them and went away once more and prayed
the third time, saying the same thing. Then he
returned to the disciples and said to them, "Are you
still sleeping and resting?"
**Matthew 26:40-41, 43-45 (NIV)**

Jesus knew the time was coming that He would have to face
His purpose for being born: death and resurrection. He knew
He needed to prepare Himself mentally for what He would
soon face, so He went to a place where He could pray. He
brought His disciples with Him requesting only two things
from them: watch and pray. He returned three times and each
time found them asleep.

Have you ever experienced this in your attempt to start
and maintain a business? You are focused and realize the
struggle that is ahead, but your employees, friends and/or
family seem to be "sleeping." You are seriously and devotedly
moving in one direction, but everyone else around you is
standing still. You call out to them, "Wake up," but they
continue to remain unaffected, unprepared, and unmotivated.

Having a vision and foresight is a lonely battle. God
reveals to you the plan and an idea of what's to come, but it
then becomes your job to communicate and explain that plan
to those in the trenches with you. Many times you have to
fight alone because others will not understand why you are

doing what you're doing or directing them the way you are directing. No matter how much you warn, guide, and train your team, you might end up at war all by yourself.

Do not be discouraged. You are never truly alone, even when it feels this way. The most important team member is there by your side, ready to take you to victory: the Lord. As the devil attempted to tempt Jesus, as His own flesh threatened to forsake Him, as His troops disobeyed him, God was present with Jesus in Gethsemane, giving Him all of the power He needed to endure His challenge.

God is also there with you. He promises to give you strength, love, peace, joy, power, and victory. When you find yourself in a Gethsemane situation, alone and overwhelmed, be like Jesus and look to the Father for everything you need to overcome.

## PRAYER

*Jesus, You understand how it feels to have foresight that those following You cannot comprehend. You have experienced the loneliness of the call. Right now, I am facing that same sense of isolation. Please be with me as I move forward into this battle. Watch over me, protect me, empower me, and lead me to victory. Help me as I deal with others who do not understand the vision. Show me how to communicate the plan to them and motivate them into action. I believe that no matter who is with me or who is not, that with You by my side, I will win this war. In Your name, Jesus. Amen.*

# THE LOVE OF MONEY

Reading: 1 Timothy 6

**People who want to get rich will fall into temptation and a trap and into many foolish and harmful desires that plunge men into ruin and destruction. For the love of money is a root of all kinds of evil. Some people, eager for money, have wandered from the faith and pierced themselves with many griefs.**
**1 Timothy 6:9-10 (NIV)**

Most new businesses do not make much money in their first few years. There are always exceptions to the rule, but entrepreneurs in general know to be conservative in their expectations. Lack of financial means makes people desperate and desperate people do desperate things. On the opposite end of the spectrum, people who already have money many times feel the need to have more, fearing that they will one day lose what they already have.

Regardless of your place on the financial status continuum, we all must be careful of our relationship with money. This passage teaches us that it is easy to be tempted by money and to fall into a path that leads to destruction and spiritual misguidance. There is nothing wrong with wanting to get paid or even accumulating monetary gain, but the more focused we become on making money, the more vulnerable we become to sin and evil.

We constantly see in the media CEOs and other high-ranking officials of large corporations being criticized for participating in illegal business acts and think to ourselves, "I would never do that." However, the reality is that at one time those very people probably felt the same way about themselves. The foundation of temptation is deceiving us to believe and justify something that is wrong. The continuous performance and rationalization of sin produces more, bigger, and deeper sin. Their wrongs may have begun small with a lie here and there to make more money, and ended with scandals that rocked the American economy.

It is easy to judge others' sin until you are placed in the same shoes and find yourself tempted as well. Instead of shaking our heads in shame at these fallen leaders behavior, let us look to their mistakes as opportunities to learn what not to do. We must think of money in the proper perspective. It is wonderful to be rewarded with monetary resources, but there is freedom, peace, and joy in receiving it in a godly manner.

As you conduct business, ask yourself these questions: Are my means for making a profit ways that God would approve? If I were a customer, would these prices and fees be fair to me? Am I doing all that I know how to do to conduct business in a legal and ethical manner? Do I consider myself a trustworthy person? Do I give with a willing heart to God? Do I put making money before God, my family, and other life priorities? Do I neglect important things in life so that I can earn more money? Can I share and give money cheerfully to others? Be honest with yourself as you answer these questions. If you find any of your answers to be leaning towards the love of money, immediately repent and ask God to help you put money in its proper place.

# PRAYER

*Creator and Holy One, I bow before You in reverence and awe. You know everything about me, all of my ways and all of my flaws. Yet You love me unconditionally and for this, I thank You. I desire to be a good leader who loves You more than anything in this world including money. I believe in You for financial blessings upon my life and my business. Help me not to become so desperate to get rich that I fall into temptation. If I care for money more that I should, forgive me and bring me into in a healthy relationship with money. Deliver me from the evil and deceptive pit of materialism and monetary gain. Let my small actions be holy and righteous so that as this business grows and expands I can continue in honesty and uprightness. Thank you, Lord, for freedom from evil. In Jesus' name. Amen.*

# THE GOOD IN THE BAD

Reading Isaiah 38

**I waited patiently till dawn, but like a lion he broke all my bones; day and night you made an end of me...You restored me to health and let me live. Surely it was for my benefit that I suffered such anguish. In your love you kept me from the pit of destruction; you have put all my sins behind your back.**
**Isaiah 38:13-17 (NIV)**

Hezekiah wrote these words after being delivered from an illness that almost took his life. Recall a time in your life when you were very sick. Think back to how bad you felt, how miserable and unhappy you were, how much the pain consumed your being. Those memories may give you a taste of what Hezekiah experienced before writing these words.

I imagine this was probably one of the most difficult times in Hezekiah's life. He waited on deliverance from God, but it seemed like it would never come. He waited for sunshine, but the dark clouds and rain would not recede. Death appeared inescapable. At the moment when all hope was lost, the Lord stepped in and healed him, giving him grace, mercy, and love. In hindsight, he testifies that the pain he endure was for his good and ultimately, God is good.

Right now, you and/or your business may be experiencing an "illness" from which recovery seems unlikely. Times may be harder than ever before, the night darker, the winds stronger. Your problem may be so large that your life is now revolving around it and failure or "death" may be inevitable.

But there is always a "but." God is still able. Like Hezekiah, He can "restore you to health and let you live." You can move from writing your obituary to writing your testimony. His love can save you from destruction and He can put all of your sins behind His back.

Whatever you are going through, it is for your benefit. When God is involved, there is always good in the bad. The "sicknesses" of life all have a purpose and push us further into the will of God. We grow, become stronger, wiser, more prepared, and more faithful to complete that good work which we were called to do.

At the end of our trials, we should be able to identify some of their benefits. What was the hardest thing you have ever endured? What did you learn from that experience? As you face today's challenges know that God will not ever put more on you than you can bear. There is purpose to your pain and good in the bad.

## PRAYER

*Lord, I can relate to Hezekiah. I am undergoing suffering like never before. I know what it feels to be made an end of, day and night. But I believe that despite what I am going through, You are here and will restore me. Let me live and save me from destruction. Let Your love pour out on my business and me. I trust that there is reason for my pain and good in the bad. You would not allow this unless it was for my benefit and Your glory. Thank You, Father, for the testimony that will result from this experience. In the name of Jesus. Amen.*

# PRAYER CHANGES THINGS

Reading: Isaiah 38

**Hezekiah turned his face to the wall and prayed to the Lord, "Remember, O Lord, how I have walked before you faithfully and with wholehearted devotion and have done what is good in your eyes." And Hezekiah wept bitterly. Then the word of the Lord came to Isaiah: Go and tell Hezekiah, "This is what the Lord, the God of your father David, says: I have heard your prayer and seen your tears; I will add fifteen years to your life."**

**Isaiah 38:2-5 (NIV)**

In this Old Testament story, we learn that King Hezekiah used prayer to get the attention of God and lengthen his life. Hezekiah was a man who allowed God to use him to lead the people in victory over their enemies. He took his cares to the Lord and the Lord always took care of him. However, in this story he becomes fatally sick and is told by the prophet Isaiah that he will not make it. Can you imagine his pain? Here is a good person getting a bad deal. It just doesn't seem fair. How many times do you feel like Hezekiah? You are trying to do the right things, live a good life, do good business, but failure and (business) death seem unavoidable.

When Hezekiah heard the news, he was devastated. But instead of losing his mind and tearing up the room in a manic fit, he does the only thing that can change his situation; he prays. His prayer is so honest and sincere God is moved to add fifteen years onto his life. I guess prayer actually does change things.

How do you respond to tragic, disappointing, or just plain bad news? Do you throw an adult temper tantrum and knock everything off your desk? Do you shoot things at the walls, yell at people who have nothing to do with your problem, or wallow in liquor and drugs? Or, do you turn to God, pouring out your heart and soul through prayer; begging the only One who has the power to divinely solve your problem for mercy and grace? Hezekiah made the right decision and his choice resulted in healing and longevity.

Whatever you are facing today, these words should encourage you. Our prayers can move God. He is able to turn our circumstances around after hearing our earnest pleas. As you experience hardships in your business, take them to the Lord. As you struggle to keep your business afloat, call upon God. As your business moves closer to a point of death, turn to God. There is hope in our prayers.

## PRAYER

*Father, I praise You that You are a God that is moved by my prayers and tears. In the past, I may not have always come to You first or may have dealt with my problems in ways that are unproductive. Help me to be someone who will come to You immediately after hearing bad news. I truly believe that my prayer changes things because of Your love for me. Hear my prayer and change (Fill in the blank.). Remember me and how I have tried to do what is right. Have mercy upon me. If You don't, I will not recover. My faith is in You God. In the name of Jesus, I pray these things. Amen.*

# WORRY-FREE

Reading: Philippians 4

**Rejoice in the Lord always, I will say it again: Rejoice! Let your gentleness be evident to all. The Lord is near. Do not be anxious about anything, but in everything, by prayer and petition, with thanksgiving, present your requests to God. And the peace of God, which transcends all understanding, will guard your hearts and minds in Christ Jesus.**
**Philippians 4:4-7 (NIV)**

Owning a business is one of the most stressful and anxiety-provoking endeavors you can pursue. By walking away from the traditional way of making money and from what I call "paycheck mentality," you place yourself in an extremely vulnerable position. Before, your biggest concern was keeping your job so that you could pay your bills; now your worries stretch as far as the sea. Will I generate a profit today? Will I make enough to pay both my personal and business expenses? Can my employees depend on my company for their survival? Will customers need my product or services? Is my advertising working? Will I go into more debt? Will I go bankrupt? These and many other questions have the potential to cloud your thoughts on a daily basis.

One day in the midst of my anxieties, God put a mirror up to me and said, "Look at you! You can't sleep at night, your body is all out-of-whack, you're depressed, and you are barely getting anything accomplished! You are stressing yourself out, worrying about everything! You trust me, but not enough for the wonderful things I have for you. This is why I am stretching your faith; to get you from endless worry to a place of peace." I had to get real with myself and admit that I was a worrier–had been all of my life. I had taken being responsible to a completely new level by becoming consumed with anxiety over my ability to make everything in my life run smoothly.

This scripture teaches us the process of receiving peace and reducing stress in our lives. First, it suggests that we should always remain in a state of joy and kindness because God is always present in our lives. Then it advises that if we do find ourselves with a need or concern that we must immediately take it to the Lord in prayer. During our prayer time, not only should we ask for what we desire, but also we should thank God for what He has already done and what we are believing in Him to do. If we are committed to following these steps, we will find ourselves in a place of peace that is not dependent on our current circumstances.

There are so many things in the world to be anxious about, but God is near. He is able to take us from fear to freedom if we would only present our requests to Him. At times of worry and stress, let us remember that He is just a prayer away.

## PRAYER

*Lord, You promise to be near and an ever present help in my time of need. I admit to allowing stress, worry, anxiety, and fear consume my thoughts, many times preventing me from being as productive as I should be. I desire to have peace that transcends all understanding. I want to live every day with joy in my heart and gentleness in my actions. I bring before You the issues that keep me stressed and present my petition to You which includes: (Fill in the blank). Please Lord, give me (Fill in the blank). I thank you for all that You have done for me already. You have blessed me in ways that I cannot communicate. I also thank You for this answered prayer, how you are going to work out this issue in my life. I praise You, Lord, for the peace that is entering into my heart and mind as I speak this prayer, and ask that it keep me calm as I wait for you to manifest my breakthrough into the natural realm. In the precious name of Jesus. Amen.*

# FROM BAD TO WORSE

Reading: 1 Samuel 28

**When Saul saw the Philistine army, he was afraid; terror filled his heart. He inquired of the Lord, but the Lord did not answer him by dreams or Urim or prophets. Saul then said to his attendants, "Find me a woman who is a medium, so I may go and inquire of her." "There is one in Endor," they said.**
**1 Samuel 28:4-7 (NIV)**

Here we witness King Saul going from a bad situation to an even worse one. He is placed in the position as king, but because he does not follow the leading of God, his anointing is given to David. He knows his time is running out. When he finds himself in a war and that his likelihood of winning is slim-to-none, he now tries to seek the Lord. However, God does not answer him.

In a moment of desperation, he seeks guidance from a medium or in today's terms a psychic. The medium ends up bringing up the spirit of Samuel who confirms that Saul will be defeated and David will take over his crown. Saul has turned his back on God and God is no longer with Saul.

Every negative circumstance in our life that is self-induced has the ability to go from bad to worse. If we disobey God, we put ourselves in a vulnerable position. Our sin can create difficult and negative consequences in our lives. As an entrepreneur, it is essential that you follow the leading of God and not your own flesh. Our carnality can get us into a lot of trouble. It is not just our careers at stake, but also our lifestyle and those of our employees that are at risk as well.

Saul unrelentingly made his circumstances worse by not repenting and continuing to do things his own way, seeking help from ungodly things and people. If you do find yourself in a bad situation because of something that you did wrong, do not make it worst by acting out of fear and desperation. Instead, take responsibility for your mistakes, repent to the Lord and persistently seek Him for guidance.

To make mistakes is natural. A wise man once told me, "The best thing you can do is make a lot of mistakes. If you're not making any mistakes, you're not taking any risks; if you're not taking any risks, you're not growing." We learn and develop as people and as leaders through our mistakes if we can learn the valuable lessons they desire to teach us. Nevertheless, in order to learn we must first admit we made a mistake then allow ourselves to assess the error for its schooling.

Never be afraid to ask for forgiveness from God. He knows we are not perfect and many times, He allows us to fall down so that He can show us His grace, mercy, and glory as He picks us back up and gives us another chance. In your time of error, do not look to anyone but Jesus. He loves you so much that despite your sins, He died and rose so that you could have multiple opportunities to get it right with Him.

## PRAYER

*God, I thank You for being so faithful to me despite my lack of faithfulness towards You. I have messed up and made many mistakes in my life, but despite these things, You continue to love and bless me. Help me not to be like Saul who made matters worse by seeking assistance from ungodly resources. In my fallen times, I look to You with repentance for salvation, guidance, and the strength needed to get back up again. Almighty, teach me the lessons in my mistakes so that I can become a better business owner, family member, friend, and Christian. In the name of Jesus, I pray. Amen.*

# ENOUGH FAITH TO MOVE

Reading: James 2:14-26

**What good is it my brother, of a man claims to have faith but has no deeds? Can such faith save him? Suppose a brother or sister is without clothes and daily food. If one of you says to him, "Go, I wish you well; keep warm and well fed," but does nothing about his physical needs, what good is it? In the same way, faith by itself, if it is not accompanied by action, is dead.**

**James 2:14-17 (NIV)**

Owning a business is a faith walk. You do not know how things are going to work out, how bills are going to be paid, where you are going to get customers, if your business will succeed; you don't know anything. All you know is that you have a vision and that God is leading you to move in faith.

Faith is more than just believing, it is acting on that belief. If you believe it is going to rain, you take an umbrella with you. If you believe you need a certain degree to obtain certain information or a particular career that you desire, you enroll in school. When you came to believe that Jesus could save you from your sins, you acted on that belief by repenting and accepting his salvation into your life. The evidence of faith is action.

In these verses from the book of James, we learn that faith without works is useless. To believe something, but not behave according to that belief is pointless. There are many things we need in order for our businesses to run smoothly, but if we are not willing to do our part in faith, God will not do His. A seed must be planted before the harvest can be achieved. We must plant the seed and water it; God will do the rest.

At the beginning of starting my business, I had nothing. No money in a reserve account, no office furniture, no clients, and no knowledge on how to start and run a business legally. Every time I took a step of faith, God brought the resource I needed to past. I looked for office space, God made sure the rent was paid; I signed the lease, God provided the funds for furniture; I made business cards, God brought the clients; I researched business law and structure, God gave me understanding. Each time I was willing to move forward despite my lack, God took that faith and action and manifested into the blessing I needed.

For those of you who want to start a business and God has given you the vision, it is now for you to begin taking at least small steps of faith. Look into the courses you will need, search the internet for business tools, create business cards, talk to other business owners, etc. Pray to God to show you the next steps to take and trust Him to move when He does.

For those who have begun a business that is still in small business status, do not become stagnant. Continue to move forward in faith to fulfill the complete vision God has given you. Get office or work space, hire employees, build your website, go further in your advertising, etc. For those whose businesses have become large companies, there are still steps of faith that you can take to bring your business to the next level; don't get so comfortable. Ask God what else you can be doing or how can you do things better. Is there a second business you can start? Can you expand and create more sites or franchise? Can you offer special or pro-bono services to needy communities? Whatever your level of entrepreneurship, have enough faith to move because faith without works is dead. Don't kill your business because you refused to move.

# PRAYER

*Heaven Father, thank You for this vision and business You have given me. Thank You for the leadership skills, management talents, and directing abilities that I possess. I believe that You will take this business that You have given to me and develop it into a successful enterprise. I believe You will touch every aspect of my business and bring increase to every area of it. You will rain down resources into it in a strong and mighty way. It shall grow and produce like never before. I believe You will transform me into a powerful person who can lead such a great company. Because I believe You will do all these things, I will move. I will step out in faith and move in the direction towards the building and maintaining of this business. I will everyday take steps of faith to show You that I truly believe in You and this business. As I move, I expect to see You move. As I do my part, I look in anticipation for You to do Yours. If I do one thing, Lord, You do ten. If I do ten things, Lord, You do one-hundred. Show me what step is next so that I can be faithful to Your leading and calling to this business. Thank You, Father, for the blessings that are a direct result of my faith and actions. In Jesus' name. Amen.*

# VISUAL DECEPTION

Reading: 2 Corinthians 5

**We walk by faith, not by sight.**
**2 Corinthians 5:7 (NIV)**

Naturally, our eyes are one of our most important body parts. If you were to lose one of your senses and given a choice which one it would be, most would agree that our eyes would probably be the least likely to go. We depend on our sight to navigate us through life. The eyes help us to identify what is around us and make choices based on the appearance of the things front of us.

Spiritually, our physical eyes are one of our biggest barriers. Because we so heavily rely on our sense of vision, it becomes hard for us to believe in the things we cannot see. The definition of faith is to hope for what we cannot see. However, most of us have become so dependent on our eyes that the idea of trusting in something that our eyes have not observed yet is extremely difficult.

The sense of sight then becomes a blessing and a curse, all at once. It is hard to believe the things we cannot see, but when we do and the miracle is finally manifested into the natural, our eyes allow us to witness the glory of God. The eyes function as both a hindrance and a support to our faith.

This seven-word verse in second Corinthians informs us so simply that sight is not the motivating factor for a Christian; faith is. Vision can be deceptive, keeping us from believing in the very words and plans of God. The enemy uses our trust in sight to prevent us from walking or moving in the will of God.

As an entrepreneur, it is essential that you walk by faith and not by sight. There will be many things that your eyes will show you that will be opposing to the word of the Lord. If you give into what you immediately see, you risk missing what you have not seen yet.

However, God gives us another kind of sight: spiritual vision. You cannot always trust what you see in the flesh, but you can always depend on what God shows you through your spiritual lenses. The word tells us to write the vision and make it plain (Habakkuk 2:2). When God gives you a vision, write it down as clearly as He gives it to you. Don't skimp on the details. You will need this written reminder when your physical eyes start to play tricks on you and suggest to you that what God told you will not come to pass. Use your eyes to confirm your beliefs. Return to your written vision and prove to your physical sight that what is being observed is not completely accurate.

Be a leader that walks by faith and not by what you see. We please God through our ability to trust Him at His word. Do not miss the promises of God because you were visually deceived. When what you see does not reflect what the Lord has revealed to you, know it is all just an optical illusion.

## PRAYER

*Omniscient God, You are the God who sees all. You are aware of my struggles with my sense of sight and how I have come to rely too much on what I see. You are a God of faith and are pleased in me when I have faith in You. Forgive me for allowing what I see to keep me from believing what You have revealed to me. Give me spiritual vision that I can cling to when my eyes attempt to deceive me. I know that if I stand in faith that every promise You've given me will come to pass. I aim to walk in faith every day. In the name of Jesus. Amen.*

# BREATHLESS

Reading: Ezekiel 37:1-14

So I prophesied as I was commanded. And as I was prophesying, there was a noise, a rattling sound, and the bones came together, bone to bone. I looked, and tendons and flesh appeared on them and skin covered them, but there was no breath in them. Then he said to me, "Prophesy to the breath; prophesy, son of man, and say to it, 'This is what the Sovereign Lord says: Come from the four winds, O breath, and breathe into these slain, that they may live.' " So I prophesied as he commanded me, and breath entered them; they came to life and stood up on their feet – a vast army.
**Ezekiel 37:7-10 (NIV)**

Sometimes, all we are lacking is breath. A second wind, new life, or fresh breath is what is needed to get us moving again. Life can be hard, and at times, downright exhausting. The weight of a heavy load, pressure from every side, and the burden of responsibility can drain every drop of energy within us, leaving us feeling like nothing more than dry bones.

It is natural at times of severe fatigue to want to give up. There will be those moments in your business building and maintaining that quitting will appear to be the best option. You may feel tired of struggling or not interested in going through the pain anymore. It may seem like taking the more conservative route, staying in the shallow end and letting others swim out into the deep, is the safer and smarter move for you to make.

To whom much is given, much is required (Luke 12:48). If you desire to experience "big things" in this life, you will have to go through some "big things." If God simply gave you everything you wanted without you having to work hard for it, you would not appreciate it and you wouldn't know how to manage it. By allowing you to endure hardships, you learn the value of your blessings and how to keep them once you have received them.

After my first year as a business owner, I felt like I had been in the position for five or ten years. I had gone through so much in that first year. God allowed me to experience success and failure, good times and hard times, growth and stagnation. I had worked with some of the best clients and some of the worst. I had made money and lost money. I paid bills and went into debt. I had smiled and cried, felt confident and afraid. As I continued to submit myself to the ups and downs of the vision, I became a stronger, wiser, and a better leader and businesswoman.

Although my tears were for my good, I also required revival. After the trials, I needed a pick-me-up, a boost to get me going again. I had run so much and so hard that I had become out of breath–breathless. Without air, we cannot survive. Without air, our businesses cannot thrive. God was there to give me the second wind that I required. He breathed into me new life when I had spent the old life in me. When you feel yourself at the point where your oxygen is so low that passing out is inevitable, ask God to breath into you. He is able to fill you up again and keep you pressing toward the mark.

## PRAYER

*Life Giver, I praise You for the life you have given me. Thank You for Your reviving abilities that have given me the strength to not give up. There are times when the days are so dark and the winter is so cold that success feels impossible. I admit that I've considered quitting or not pursuing the vision the way You are directing me to do. In these times, remind me of the call and breathe fresh air into me. Give me a second, third, and even a fourth wind so that I can continue on the road of entrepreneurship. I am made new as You breathe into me. In the name of Jesus, I pray. Amen.*

# THE BEST REVENGE

Reading: Psalm 64

**They shoot from ambush at the innocent man; they shoot at him suddenly, without fear. They encourage each other in evil plans, they talk about hiding their snares; they say, "Who will see them?" They plot injustice and say, "We have devised a perfect plan!" Surely the mind and heart of man are cunning. But God will shoot them with arrows; suddenly they will be struck down. He will turn their own tongues against them and bring them to ruin; all those who see them will shake their heads in scorn.**
**Psalm 64:4-8 (NIV)**

Success is the best revenge and the greatest vindicator is the Lord. We all have found ourselves at one time or another at the end of someone's vicious plot. People don't like us for various reasons, some that make sense and some that do not. Because of jealousy, fear, and hate, people conjure up schemes to bring us down and ruin the very things we have worked so hard to create.

David was no exception. In this psalm, he writes about how his enemies are planning for his demise. They evilly conspire to hurt him; they say harsh words in attempts to damage his reputation. They think their plans are so perfect and that nothing can stop them from bringing him down. But David knew better. He knew that he served a God who was omniscient, omnipotent, and omnipresent. God would vindicate him and protect him from the snares of malicious people.

Not only would God protect him, but God would also use their malevolent tactics against them. The very words they used against David would be used against them. The very arrows they aimed at David would be aimed back at them.

Have you ever witnessed the vindication of the Lord? Have you ever experienced someone coming against you and ending up being caught in his or her own trap? Have you ever seen that very person that tried to mistreat you, being mistreated? If you have, you already know how much better God is at vengeance than we are.

As a business owner, people will not always like you. Some may purposely aim to hurt you through lies, deceit, trickery, and physical harm. If you focus on warring with these people, your attention is no longer directed towards your goals. Your enemies win because you cannot accomplish the things for which they are jealous. However, if you continue focusing on the vision and leave vindication to the Lord, He will protect, defend, and uplift you. The best revenge is letting God be your vindicator.

## PRAYER

*Emmanuel, You are with me at all times. I know that even when people plot against me, You are aware of their schemes and they will not prevail. Help me to remain focused on my goals, even when it seems as if my enemies are closing in on me. Fight my battles Lord; I submit my right to revenge to You. I know that vengeance belongs to You and that you can work things out in ways that I cannot fathom. Thank You for protecting and redeeming me. In the name of Jesus Christ. Amen.*

# EMPLOYEE BENEFITS

Reading: Colossians 3:18-4:6

**Masters, provide your slaves with what is right and fair, because you know that you also have a Master in heaven.**
**Colossians 4:1 (NIV)**

Think back to when you were an employee. Some of you may have to think back further than others. Some of you still may be an employee. What were your experiences being employed by someone else? How were you treated? Was your pay fair? Were your achievements recognized? Was the environment peaceful or chaotic? Were your concerns taken seriously? Were your ideas appreciated or considered? How did your treatment as an employee influence your company loyalty? How did it affect your decision to work for yourself?

Many of us became an entrepreneur because of poor treatment as an employee. We were tired of being underemployed, underpaid, overworked, and overlooked. We wanted to be appreciated, valued, praised, and acknowledged. We wanted respect, promotion, and positive attention. We wanted to feel indispensable, needed, and secure. However, many employers did not meet our career needs and left us feeling that we had no other choice than to go out on our own. For those of us who are successful entrepreneurs, we are glad that our negative experiences led us to a place of ownership and freedom. For those of us who are struggling with self-employment, we sometimes wish our former employers had made life more comfortable for us so that we could have maintained employee status.

Now being in the position of an employer, it is time for you to choose what type of employer you will be. Will you be like your old supervisors and managers, pushing your employees to seek work elsewhere? Or, will you be the employer that you always wanted to have when you were an employee, someone that will not make work harder than it already is, someone who will recognize talent and cherish a hard worker, someone who creates loyalty and community among their employees?

In the verse above, the words master and slave are used to define a relationship of superior to subordinate or submission to a higher authority. We are instructed to treat those that are underneath our command justly. We are directed to do what is right in relation to those who work for us. We are warned to remember that we too are subjected to the power of another. God is our superior, even when we don't have an earthly employer.

As you employ others, treat them the way you want to be treated. Bless them with the monetary and non-monetary benefits that you can afford and that they deserve. Your goodness toward your employees will be rewarded by your heavenly employer: God. In addition, you will save money by reducing high turnover rates and build a sense of loyalty among your staff.

## PRAYER

*God, You are my Master and I submit myself to You. I have experienced poor treatment as an employee and I do not want to make my staff feel the negative emotions that I've felt. Help me to be good to my subordinates and to do what is right by them. Grant me favor and blessings so that that I can pay them fairly. Show me ways that I can strengthen them through respect, acknowledgement, and promotion. Assist me as I create an environment that produces loyalty, community, and peace. In the name of Jesus, I ask these things. Amen.*

# DON'T GIVE UP

Reading: Galatians 6

**Do not be deceived; God is not mocked. A man reaps what he sows. The one who sows to please his sinful nature, from that nature will reap destruction; the one who sows to please the Spirit, from the Spirit will reap eternal life. Let us not become weary in doing good, for at the proper time we will reap a harvest if we do not give up.**
**Galatians 6:7-9 (NIV)**

There is a harvest. I will say it again; there is a harvest. You may really need to hear these words. You may have been sowing for a long time. You may have put everything you have and don't have into your business, praying that it would be enough. You may have planted the seed, watered it daily, but come out every day just to find nothing growing. You search the soil for some hope, a speck of green, anything to let you know that your hard work has not been in vain. Yet the ground is empty and you walk away feeling defeated.

But there is a harvest. God's word promises us that we will reap what we sow. But before you get too excited, the question becomes; what are you sowing and what is the motivation behind your sowing? Bad seed and wrong motivation will produce a bad and wrong harvest. If you plant seeds that replicates sin such as being consumed by money, cheating people, lying, stealing, burning bridges, scheming, conniving, selfish, or any other negative behavior or trait, your fruit will reflect these characteristics. Your customers will behave this way and your path will lead to destruction. However, if your seed reflects the things of God such as goodness, kindness, faithfulness, fairness, honesty, or any other positive behavior or trait, your fruit will mirror these good things.

Harvest will come if we do not give up. Giving up is a very real option that is presented to us daily. "Now Hiring" signs and paychecks dance in front of our eyes, tempting us to let go of this silly dream and just be like everyone else. Friends and family–the main ones who should be supporting us–place fear in us by giving us their opinions and advice. Creditors remind us of our dry season by sending us threatening letters and harassing phone calls. Everything around us yells, "Give up! You can't do it! Stop now before you lose it all!" And some of us crumble. Some of us walk away from the one thing that made us feel alive. Some of us get weary.

The bible tells us not to allow ourselves to get tired of doing what is right because if we hold out, there is a harvest. You may feel exhausted, but hold out. You may feel depleted, but hold on. You may feel alone, beat down, frustrated, drained, or lower than you have ever felt, but hold tight. Harvest is coming if you don't give up.

## PRAYER

*King of Kings and Lord of Lords, usher me into Your presence. At times, I want to give up because the weight of this vision is a heavy load to bear. But Your word tells me not to let go because harvest will come. It tells me that I will see the fruit of my sowing; that I will reap, my labor is not in vain. When things of this world come to place fear in me and rob me of my peace, I ask that You keep me and give me joy and tranquility. Let my seeds be those that are of the Spirit so that life can be produced in my harvest. Thank You, Father. In the blessed name of Jesus. Amen.*

# YOU GOTTA EAT

Reading: 2 Thessalonians 3

**For you yourselves know how you ought to follow our example. We were not idle when we were with you, not did we eat anyone's food without paying for it. On the contrary, we worked night and day, laboring and toiling so that we would not be a burden to any of you We did this, not because we do not have the right to such help, but in order to make ourselves a model for you to follow. For even when we were with you, we gave you this rule: "If a man will not work, he shall not eat."**
**2 Thessalonians 3:7-10 (NIV)**

We work because we need to survive. We have bills to pay and mouths to feed. Our income from working allows us to provide for our families and ourselves. Most people work for others because it is the easier route to generating the funds needed to live.

Business owners are those people who understand the importance of working for survival, but at the same time feel they have something more to offer society than just clocking in. They care about making ends meet, yet they are willing to risk instant financial gratification in efforts to gain long-term monetary gains and inner fulfillment.

The purpose of working, rather it be for a company or for yourself, is to make enough or more than enough money to handle living expenses. However, one of the biggest challenges for new entrepreneurs is how to charge people for their products or services. If you are a good person who is not "money-hungry" you may find yourself wrestling with making people pay the prices you deserve to get paid.

If you own a business that sells products, this may not be as difficult because you possibly have selling guidelines and suggested retail pricing. You still could find yourself debating on whether to sell your product closer to the retail price or closer to the wholesale price. Selling at the retail price will generate better revenue, but selling lower could drive more business your way due to the discount.

If you own a business the sells a service, pricing issues become stickier. You need to charge customers a rate that is fair and beneficial to them however, you also need to make a profit and sell your service at a rate that is best for you. Regardless of your type of business, the bottom line when it comes to pricing is value.

You have to value yourself, your business, and your products or services. If you do not, no one else will. Your rates will determine the value you place on what you are selling. We don't value things we buy from the dollar store because we only paid a dollar for them. We value expensive designer clothing because we pay a whole lot for it. For example, I've owned dozens of sunglasses in my life and usually they end up lost or scratched up because I leave them anywhere, don't put them in their cases, drop them, throw them haphazardly in my purse, and treat them any kind of way. However, one day I purchased a pair of Chanel sunglasses. $425 plus tax. I almost cried when I first put them one because they were so fierce! I had never spent over $30 for shades before this so buying these glasses was huge for me. The glasses became like a rare and precious stone in my mind. I always placed them in their case when I wasn't wearing them, hardly ever left them in my car, I didn't even want to put them on top of my head because I didn't want my hair to get the lenses oily. I valued my shades because the maker, Chanel, values them enough to put a large price tag on them.

Now I am not encouraging you to make your products or services ridiculously expensive, but I am suggesting that you determine your target audience and price your business accordingly. You have to value what you do or others will not value you, causing you to not make money. One of the main goals of working is to make money. No matter who is your customer, unless you have a business that offers free services, you have to charge so that you can make a profit. Remember, you gotta eat.

## PRAYER

*Lord, I come to You for wisdom and knowledge on how to run my business appropriately and effectively. I sometimes struggle with my prices, not knowing what is fair to both my customer and me. Please guide me on what my rates should be. Help me not to be motivated by money, but understand that this is a business and I have needs too. Help me to value what I do and place value on my products and services so that others will respect my business. I praise You for insight and discretion. In the name of Christ Jesus. Amen.*

# NAKEDNESS

Reading: Romans 8

**Who shall separate us from the love of Christ? Shall trouble or hardship or persecution or famine or nakedness or danger or sword? As it is written: "For your sake we face death all day long; we are considered as sheep to be slaughtered." No, in all these things we are more than conquerors through him that loved us.**
**Romans 8:35-37 (NIV)**

Starting and running a business can put you in an extremely vulnerable position. At times, it may seem as if you are naked and exposed, the whole world witnessing the weakest parts of you. For so long we have attempted to hide behind money, prestige, intellect, fancy clothing, flashy jewels, and an aura of strength. Now we lay uncovered, stripped of all that would conceal us, bare for all to see who we really are.

When you are an employee you can hide behind the company you work for, but when you're the employer, who is there to protect you? You become the fish in the clear, glass fishbowl, on display for anybody to watch you, a constant state of nakedness. Some of us enjoy the limelight, whether it is positive or negative; others of us abhor it. Yet, most of us would agree that being on a pedestal that is falling apart is not a comfortable place to be.

Regardless of how vulnerable we feel or how difficult our journey to entrepreneurship is we can be sure that there is a place of comfort and security. Who can separate us from the love of Christ? Nothing and nobody! No matter if our business succeeds or fails, God continues to love us and shower us with His unconditional, unexplainable love.

Sometimes as a Christian business owner, you will experience hardships just because what is in the world does not want you to achieve what is for Christ. Distractions will consume you–problems and issues that have nothing and everything to do with your calling. You will wake up motivated and go to sleep frustrated. Just when peace enters your mind, a phone call, a letter, or some other method of sabotage will appear, chasing your soundness away.

Nevertheless, nothing can separate us from the love of Christ. That is a guarantee. If we lose everything, we still have Christ. His love brings us through the toughest circumstances and labels us as survivors. We can and will make it to conquering status. Not only will we triumph over our hardships, but also our victory will be in abundance. We are more than conquerors.

Today, tell your bills you are more than a conqueror. Tell your unbelieving relatives, you are more than a conqueror. Tell your enemies you are more than a conqueror. Tell your fear and doubt you are more than a conqueror. Because He loves us, He will save us and nothing can stand between us and the love of our God.

## PRAYER

*God, You are love, and I thank You for Your endless love for me. I praise You that no matter who or what tries to steal Your love away, it is impossible. Nothing can come between us. Nothing can separate me from Your love. No matter what I am experiencing or feeling, today I hold on to my relationship with You. I know that after the winds have blown and the rain has fallen that I will survive this thing. I will have the victory because I am more than a conqueror through You. In the name of Jesus. Amen.*

# IT'S NOT ABOUT ME

Reading: Romans 9

For he says to Moses, "I will have mercy on whom I have mercy, and I will have compassion on whom I have compassion." It does not depend on man's desire or effort, but on God's mercy. For the Scripture says to Pharaoh: "I raised you up for this very purpose, that I might display my power in you and that my name might be proclaimed in all the earth." Therefore God has mercy on whom he wants to have mercy, and he hardens whom he wants to harden.
**Romans 9:15-18 (NIV)**

How successful you are as a business owner is not about you. Favor will be granted to you depending on the will of God. We are taught that hard work by itself leads to the blessings of the Lord. However, God's favor in your life has nothing to do with how much you deserve it; it has to do with His mercy and His glory.

We have come to believe that God exists in our lives to make us happy and give us the things we want. We are extremely disappointed when things do not go our way, even when we are doing what is right. The perfect example of this is in the life of Job.

Job was a good man in whom God was very pleased. God was so pleased with him that when the devil came around looking for someone to tempt, God offered up Job. Everything important to Job was taken away from him. His friends and family thought he must have done something wrong. We think, "If I am doing everything right, shouldn't I be the last person to suffer?"

Still God will have mercy on whom He wants to. God made a living sacrifice out of Job. God's glory was revealed through Job's sorrow and salvation.

This life is not all about us, despite our misguided thinking. It is about God. He will use whomever He wants to get His glory. We may not understand His ways, but we are wise if we learn to accept them.

Some people get chance after chance to get it right. Other people are ruined after one bad mistake. Some people have everything and deserve nothing. Others deserve everything, yet have nothing. It all seems unjust.

God's word remains the same. He will have mercy and compassion on whom He chooses. No need to complain and sulk about how unfair things are. If we embrace the truth that it is all about Him, fairness will no longer be an issue. If He elevates me, fine. It's all for his glory. If He keeps me at the bottom, that's okay too. It was never about me from the beginning. This is one of the hardest truths to accept, but once we do, we are free to appreciate and enjoy the life He has for us.

## PRAYER

*Lord, You are God and all of this is for You. Many times, I have not understood my pain because I have believed that You existed for my pleasure. Now I see that it is I that exist for Your pleasure. I desire to be fulfilled in this life. I want to experience success in my business, but ultimately, it is Your call. I surrender my misconceptions about this life to You. I present myself as a living sacrifice to You. Have Your way in me. In Christ Jesus' name. Amen.*

# KNOW THY LIMITATIONS

Reading: Romans 14

**Accept him whose faith is weak, without passing judgment on disputable matters. One man's faith allows him to eat everything, but another man, whose faith is weak, eats only vegetables.**
**Romans 14:1-2 (NIV)**

There is a popular saying: "Everything ain't for everybody." The wisdom of this adage is understanding that what's right and good for me may not be right and good for others, and vice versa. Each of us has to take the time to get to know ourselves so that we can make appropriate decisions for ourselves, based on the knowledge we have about ourselves.

Many times this seems unfair. One woman may be able to eat all the junk food in the world without ever gaining a pound, while another woman can't even look at chocolate without her dress size increasing. One man can be around women all day and not feel lustful or tempted, while another man can't even see a picture of a pretty woman without being overcome with lust. What I can do sometimes you cannot and what you can do sometimes I cannot.

Everyone has a weakness. Because of our flesh, we are imperfect. Our flaws make us special, unique, and keep us from being cookie cutter human beings. It is through our downfalls that God reveals our limitations to us and displays his lack of restrictions. He is able to do for us what we cannot do for ourselves.

In your business development, you may find yourself with boundaries, confines, things that you cannot do. You may struggle with these limitations both on the spiritual and natural level. There may be a certain sin that you wrestle with and have to put up walls around yourself to protect you from yourself. There might be a physical weakness, a lack of smarts, a handicap, or a lack of resources. Whatever your limitation, God has the power to help you rise above that thing.

If you see a brother or sister in Christ struggling with a limitation, do not judge them. It is easy to point out others problems without even attempting to help them. It is also simple to become a roadblock to them, enticing them to fall deeper into their weakness. Instead of becoming a part of the problem, be a part of the solution. Teach them what you know, share with them your weakness so that the two of you may support each other. Pray for them, listen to them, and help steer them away from their temptations. It may not be fair that we have to deal with limitations, but it is a blessing that God can free us from every constraint.

## PRAYER

*Mighty One, who has no limitations, I thank You for being my source of liberation. There are things that I struggle with both spiritually and naturally. Please deliver me from my limitations, or if not, help me to overcome them. Where there are weaknesses in my business, I lift them up to You and ask for Your assistance in correcting these problems. When I see another dealing with a shortcoming, help me not to be judgmental, but loving, accepting, and understanding. Let my light shine so that I am not a stumbling block, but instead a reminder that there is help in You, God. In the glorious name of Jesus. Amen*

# HALF CRAZY

Reading: Romans 7

**For what I do is not the good I want to do; no the evil I do not want to do-this I keep on doing...For in my inner being I delight in God's law; but I see another law at work in the members of my body, waging war against the law of my mind and making me a prisoner of the law of sin at work within my members. What a wretched man I am? Who will rescue me from this body of death? Thanks be to God-through Jesus Christ our Lord!**

**Romans 7:20-25 (NIV)**

Paul, the writer of this text, may seem somewhat crazy as he describes his internal struggle, but this is one of the most honest passages in the bible. The truth is that we are all half crazy. Like Paul, we face a war within ourselves, a battle over our minds.

We want to be good people: good business owners, good family members, good friends, good Christians. We even try our hardest to do what is right and what is pleasing to God. Even in our best efforts, we fall short. The sinful nature in us convinces us to do the things that we know are most damaging to our relationship with God.

This entire back and forth, good and evil war is staged in our mind. It is a real fight, a real battle, but it is a spiritual altercation that first occurs within us, with the results seeping out into our natural behaviors. The flesh is powerful and if we are not in top spiritual shape, we will find ourselves like Paul, a prisoner to sin.

How does this impact the lives of entrepreneurs? You may want to do what's right, but you find yourself operating your business in ungodly or illegal ways. Cheating at taxes, operating without certain licenses, unfair rates, dishonesty, stealing, overworking, inappropriate relationships with staff or customers, need I go on?

As Christians, the law of God is written in our hearts. We truly want to do what is right, but the law of sin is also within us and many times we find ourselves doing the very opposite of what we would like to do. We find ourselves doing what we hate. In the end, we feel like a madman. Half crazy. Paul called himself a wretched man. But thanks be to God because we do have a choice. He is able to keep us from falling if we allow Him to. Seek Him daily for the strength to win the war within you.

## PRAYER

*Holy God, You are without blemish and without spot. I truly desire to be more like You, but daily I war with myself. The sin in me wants to control me and keep me in captivity. You are the only one who can protect me from myself. Free me from every thought and act that does not reflect who You are. Change me so that I love what is right and only do those things. Help me to live holy even as I deal with my business interactions. Forgive me for falling and let Your grace give me another chance. You are the Lamb of God which takes away all of my sin. In the name of Jesus, I pray. Amen.*

# A CHANGE OF PLAN

Reading: Esther 2

**Mordecai had a cousin named Hadassah, whom he had brought up because she had neither father nor mother. This girl, who was also known as Esther, was lovely in for and features, and Mordecai has taken her as his own daughter when her father and mother died. When the king's order and edict had been proclaimed, many girls were brought to the citadel of Susa and put under the care of Hegai. Esther also was taken to the king's palace and entrusted to Hegai, who had charge of the harem.**
**Esther 2:7-8 (NIV)**

Hadassah (or Esther) had to on more than one occasion deal with a change of plan. First, she probably planned to grow up in a home with her parents, but these plans were altered when her parents died and left her in the care of her cousin Mordecai. Then she probably planned to live her life amongst her people, the Jews. This plan was also ruined when she was taken to the king's palace to eventually become his wife, the queen. Finally, once she became queen she figured she never have to expose herself as a Jew. Wrong again. To save her people she had to risk herself and reveal her ethnicity to the king.

Esther's life is a great example of how our plans are altered by God's plan. We plot out the details of our lives and how we think things should go. The Lord comes around with His own agenda and changes our course. A change in plan can be frustrating, but if we allow God to have His way, His plans are always so much better than our own.

Owning a business and pursuing the vision God has given you is all about being open to change. So many times your road will be detoured and you will have no other choice, but to go with the flow. Customers will pull out at the last minute, employees will quit, locations will change, prices and rates will adjust, and unexpected issues will come out of nowhere. Your first inclination will be to panic. If you depend on life to go a certain way and it does not, you may get nervous.

A change in plans reflects God's desire to do something greater in your life. Do not be afraid or avoid paradigm shifts. New paths and directions lead to greater purpose. Esther accepted the greater purpose in her life to be a utensil of deliverance. What could the Lord be trying to accomplish through your life if you would only submit yourself to change?

Expect a change of plan. Wear your clothes loosely. Never get stuck or set in one way of doing things. You will constantly find yourself disappointed as God tries to redirect you onto the path He has created just for you. Instead, throw your head back, raise your hands in acceptance, and tell the Lord, "Thy will be done."

## PRAYER

*Father God, I trust that You have an amazing plan for my life. I have mapped out many things that I want for myself, but I know Your ways are not my ways. I lay every plan that I have for my life at your feet. Whatever You want, whenever you want it, I am available to You. I embrace the changes You are making I my life. I know that You know what is best for me. In Jesus' name Jesus. Amen.*

# WHO'S GOT YOUR BACK?

Reading: Ruth 1

At this they wept again. Then Orpah kissed her mother-in-law good-bye, but Ruth clung to her. "Look," said Naomi, "your sister-in-law is going back to her people and her gods. Go back with her." But Ruth replied, "Don't urge me to leave you or to turn back from you. Where you go I will go, and where you stay I will stay. Your people will be my people and your God my God. Where you die I will die, and there I will be buried. May the Lord deal with me, be it ever so severely, if anything but death separates you and me."

**Ruth 1:14-17 (NIV)**

The relationship between Ruth and Naomi is a very rare one. People who are loyal and committed are hard to find. Ruth, like her sister-in-law Orpah, could have easily taken the selfish route and went back to her people to find comfort and security. She could have even put herself in a position to remarry by going back as Naomi advised her. However, Ruth decided that best place for her to be was with her mother-in-law. She was not interested in going back to old things.

There are many reasons that could have kept Ruth from leaving Naomi. Maybe she loved her so much that the thought of leaving her was too painful. Possibly, she knew Naomi was hurting after losing her family and simply wanted to remain there to comfort her. Perhaps she had some bad experiences with her own people and did not want to return to a negative situation. Possibly she had experienced such goodness and light with Naomi that she never wanted to be separated from her. Regardless of Ruth's rationale, she refused to leave Naomi's side.

We all need people in our lives like Ruth, and we all need to be a Ruth to someone else. Entrepreneurs need loyal people that are going to be there no matter what. Before we reach a place of success, we go through "the trenches." Trenches are the times when money is low or nonexistent and the risks are overwhelming. They are the times when you wear eleven or twelve different hats at once; you are human resources, accounts payable, president, vice president, office manager, marketing, the sales representative, janitorial services, public relations, and the receptionist. These are the times when prayer and faith are the only resources you have abundance of and if you lose one of them your ship will surely sink. When you are in the trenches, Ruths are invaluable. Most people will walk away and abandon you to handle the world alone. Ruths will stay with you, pray with you, ride with you, and die with you.

So who is the Ruth in your life? Who's got your back? If you don't have anyone that you can count on, you might be selecting the wrong people to be a part of your inner circle. We all need someone who is dependable. God never intended for us to be an island.

Who can say that you are their Ruth? As much as you need to have a Ruth, you also need to be one. Maybe the reason that no one has your back is because you are too selfish to have anyone else's back. Sometimes you have to give what you really need in order to obtain it.

Be sure to appreciate the Ruths in your life. As you build your business, it will be those people who will help you achieve your vision. Moreover, remember to be a Ruth to someone else. It is your faithfulness that will aid them in reaching their dreams.

## PRAYER

*Thank You, Lord, for the people in my life that have proven to be loyal and faithful friends. Thank You that I don't have to pursue the vision alone, but instead, I have people that will go through the trenches with me. Bless them Lord for their faithfulness to me. Help me to give the same goodness they have given me to others. Let me be loyal and faithful to someone else who really needs a true friend. In the name that is above all others, Jesus Christ. Amen.*

# CRAZY FAITH

Reading: Genesis 6 & 7

So make yourself an ark of cypress wood; make rooms in it and coat it with pitch inside and out...Noah did everything just as God commanded him.

**Genesis 6:14, 22**

The Lord said to Noah, "Go into the ark, you and your whole family, because I have found you righteous in this generation...And Noah did all that the Lord commanded him.

**Genesis 7:1, 5 (NIV)**

Noah had what we in the church call "crazy faith." Crazy faith is when you are willing to trust God at all costs. It's more than just believing or even acting on that belief. It is when you are willing to go beyond the minimum action required, because you believe so strongly. When someone has crazy faith, they do more than just step out into it, they jump into it then start running.

Noah and the ark is another familiar Old Testament bible story. God tells Noah to build an ark because He is going to destroy the earth with water. God gives him specific directions on what the ark should look like and who or what should be inside it. Building the ark had to take a long time and I am sure Noah looked like a complete fool. There were probably many times that he thought to himself, "Am I really sure this is what God told me to do?" Despite his fears, others opinions, or even the grandness of this endeavor, Noah did all that God commanded him.

How many of us would be that faithful? To truly answer this question we must take an honest look at our lives and the areas of it that God has given us commands. What is the thing, the vision, the task that God has given you to do? What is it that the Lord has spoken for you to accomplish that barely makes sense to you and requires so much more than you currently possess? The bible never said that Noah was an architect or boat designer. Maybe he had built some things in his time, but never anything so huge. Do you feel like Noah? Do you feel like God has given you something to do that is so much greater than you imagined for yourself? Is your vision so unique or nonconforming that others think you are simply daydreaming?

If you are going to accomplish something spectacular in your life, you will need more than just faith, you will need crazy faith. You need faith that gets you up every morning and gets you to the office even though you do not have any customers. You need faith that makes business card, brochures, signs, flyers, and other forms of advertisement even when the market is bad. When everyone around you is nervous about money and about the economy, you need faith that sets you free from worry and moves toward your mission regardless. God is not limited to anything in this world. Crazy faith knows that. There are varying levels of faith: no faith, little faith, some faith, a lot of faith, and crazy faith. What type of faith do you have?

## PRAYER

*Thank You, Father, for the vision You've given me. Sometimes it is hard to understand what You are doing or how this thing is going to come to past, but I do believe that You will do everything You promised. Help me to have more than regular faith. I want crazy faith like Noah. I want to be able to leap out in faith to accomplish the task You've set before me. I want to trust You at all costs. Even if I look foolish to others, I know what You have commanded me and I will follow You all the way. By faith and in the name of Your Son Jesus, I pray. Amen.*

# PAY ATTENTION

Reading: Isaiah 43:14-28

**"Forget the former things; do not dwell on the past. See, I am doing a new thing! Now it springs up; do you not perceive it? I am making a way in the desert and streams in the wasteland."**
**Isaiah 43:18-19 (NIV)**

Occasionally, we go through a hardship for so long that when our change finally comes, we don't realize it. We become numb, desensitized, and in a coma like state. We stop paying attention because we stop expecting something new.

While we are suffering, our minds attempt to protect us by creating defense mechanisms to deal with the pain. As great as these methods are while we are in a difficult position, they can become barriers once we are in a better place. These mechanisms are so unconsciously ingrained into our thinking that we either don't realize they exist or we have a hard time shutting them off. If we do not terminate these thoughts and behaviors, they will work against us, sabotaging our success.

In these verses in Isaiah, the Lord is speaking to Israel and telling them that if they don't wake up and pay attention, they will miss what God is doing. God was changing their situation, giving them the deliverance they had been praying for, making a way out of no way, yet they were oblivious to it.

We also run the same risk, God blessing us and us not being able to perceive it. God is growing your business, but you continue to label it as a small business or start-up. God is making sure your bills are paid, but you tell people you are struggling. God is bringing you resources, but you are too afraid to use them because you don't want to lose them. God brings you an employee you can trust, but you treat them with skepticism because of the last person who hurt you.

The Lord is saying to you, "Forget the former things!" Do you know how powerful that is? He's telling you to let go of everything from your past that held you down. Everything you have been through, every tear you've cried, everyone who did you harm, let it all go. "I am doing a new thing! Don't you see it? In the middle of your difficulty, I am blessing you, restoring you, healing you, saving you. Pay attention!"

We have to wake up from our sleep; get up from our comas. Although the road has been rough, God is transforming our situations right in front of us. Our eyes are blurry because of all the things we've been doing to protect ourselves, but the Almighty is here now telling us to look and see. Look harder, don't you perceive it?

## PRAYER

*My God, who makes a way in the desert and streams in the wasteland. I praise You for the new things you are doing in my life and in my business. I admit I have not always noticed You in the midst of my pain. But You have been here and now You are telling me to let go of my past. I give You every former thing that has held me in captivity. I subject myself to this new dawn, this new day, this new thing You are doing in me. By faith, in the name of Jesus, I receive the new thing that is springing up in me. Amen.*

# IDENTIFY THE PROBLEM

Reading: Nehemiah 1

**Hanani, one of my brothers, came from Judah with some other men, and I questioned them about the Jewish remnant that survived the exile, and also about Jerusalem. They said to me, "Those who survived the exile and are back in the province are in great trouble and disgrace. The wall of Jerusalem is broken down, and its gates have been burned with fire." When I heard these things, I sat down and wept. For some days I mourned and fasted and prayed before the God of heaven.**
**Nehemiah 1:2-4 (NIV)**

Starting a business should be about identifying a problem and offering a solution. Nehemiah finds out that the walls and gates of Jerusalem have been destroyed and the people are in distress. He is so moved by the problem that he cries, fasts, and prays for days over it.

What issues have you in tears? What news have you heard that makes you want to pray? Over what problem would you give up food? Passion is required for a great business and identifying a problem that sparks your passion is a must. During the course of starting and maintaining a company, you will get tired, frustrated, and exhausted. You will consider quitting and going back to being an employee. It is at these times that your passion for what you do will be the encouragement you need to hang in there. You will remember the problem and how you felt when you first identified it. You will recall the emotion that it provoked in you. Your passion to be a part of the solution will refuse to allow you to give up.

So what is the problem in your neighborhood? In your church? In your community? In your country? In this world?

Luckily and unfortunately for us that want to be business owners, there are many issues that need to be resolved. God has granted you with unique talents, skills, and gifts to help you change your identified problem. Look to these traits to understand what concerns may be for you to address. If you are good with explaining difficult concepts to people your business might be in education, coaching, or ministry. If you are excellent at comforting people your business may involve counseling, health care, funeral services, or hospitality. Maybe you are great with your hands and building, repairing, or creative arts are your thing. Possibly, you have a way with words and legal services, politics, public relations, or marketing is the field for you.

Whatever your strengths are, identify problems in the world that need your abilities to fix them. Pull from your passion to get you going and keep you moving. There is a reason your heart breaks when you hear about certain issues. There is a reason that you care about matters that no one else does.

## PRAYER

*Thank You, God that the strings of my heart are pulled by the problems of this world. I am affected and drawn to do something about issues in my community, nation, and world. I bless Your name for the talents and gifts You've given me that will assist me in working towards a solution. Guide me to the areas in this world that You want me to be active and help me to identify the things that concern You. Let me be passionate about my work so that I won't give up when times get hard. I pray these things in the name of Christ Jesus. Amen.*

# THE RIGHT WAY

Reading: Nehemiah 2

**The king said to me, "What is it you want?" Then I prayed to the God of heaven, and I answered the king, "If it pleases the king and if your servant has found favor in his sight, let him send me to the city of Judah where my fathers are buried so that I can rebuild it."**
**Nehemiah 2:4-5 (NIV)**

Once you have identified the problem that you feel led to fix, it is then time to make efforts towards the solution. Nehemiah identified that his problem and passion was to rebuild the walls and gates of Jerusalem. After going to the Lord and getting the okay from God, he then went to the king to get permission from him. Nehemiah already had God's go ahead, but he still respected the law of the land and received approval from his earthly leader and employer before proceeding.

Nehemiah demonstrates for us how to pursue our plans the right way. Just because we feel there is something God has called us to do, does not mean that we're supposed to take on the Malcolm X philosophy, "By any means necessary." There is a time and place to go against the rules, but most times, that is not the first step.

Nehemiah does three things that are important to take note of. First, he prays and talks to God about his desires and plans. You must make going to God your priority. By doing so, you are sure to stay within His will. Second and thirdly, he asks for the king's permission. The king plays dual roles for Nehemiah. One, he is his employer, and two he represents the law. It is not a bad idea to talk to your employer about moving on to pursue your own endeavor. This person is a leader or business owner himself or herself and may have some good advice to pass on to you. In addition, you don't want to "burn bridges" so it is wise to be honest about your future plans. As you plan and implement your business, you will also have to get permission from the law to operate. Business licenses, permits, insurances, leases, and organization/operation agreements are all forms of obtaining permission from the law to maintain a business.

Yes it would be easier to just open shop without getting so much approval, but in the long run you will run into less opposition and problems if you get permission at the beginning. Imagine if Nehemiah would have just left and started building the wall without consulting with God and the king first. What kinds of issues could have resulted from his impulsiveness?

As you begin and maintain your business, aim to do it the right way. It may take a little longer and cost you a few more dollars, but you will feel much more secure about your company if you've taken care of the minor details first. There is a right and wrong way to do everything; which way will you do it?

## PRAYER

*Holy One, I seek You first for advisement and approval to begin and maintain my business. If You say, "Go," then I know it is the best thing for me. Help me to run my business the right way. Give me the knowledge, resources, and favor that need to gain the permission to move forward according the law of the land that I live in. Let advice and wisdom come from the mouths of my former employers so that I can avoid costly mistakes. I thank You for directing my path as I move forward in Your name, Jesus. Amen.*

# CREATE AN ENTOURAGE

Reading: Nehemiah 3

**Eliashib the high priest and his fellow priests went to work and rebuilt the Sheep Gate...The Fish Gate was rebuilt by the sons of Hassenaah...The Jeshanah Gate was repaired by Joiada son of Paseah and Meshullam son of Besodeiah...The Valley Gate was repaired by Hunun and the residents of Zanoah...The Dung Gate was repaired by Malkijah son of Recab, ruler of the district of Beth Hakkerem...The Fountain Gate was repaired by Shallun son of Col-Hozeh, ruler of the district of Mizpah.**
**Nehemiah 3 (NIV)**

Once Nehemiah received permission from the king to go work on rebuilding the walls and gates of Jerusalem, he then established a crew to help him. As described in the third chapter of Nehemiah, many men assisted him in restoring the broken down city. What is even more interesting is that each group of men was assigned a specific gate or area to repair.

As you move towards entrepreneurship, you will quickly learn that you need to create an entourage. If your vision is a big one, you cannot do it alone. You will need people who agree with what you are doing to assist you in making the dream reality.

As you establish your team, realize that different people will be best suited for different tasks. Talk to your crew about what strengths and skills they have to offer and how it can fit into your goals. Someone maybe good with answering phones, another maybe great with numbers and money, someone else might be convincing in sales. A good leader knows how to delegate responsibility to the right people.

What is also important to understand is that there are three types of people in an entourage that you will need. The first type is your support system. These people probably will not work for you or even in your industry. These are your family and friends who love you and support what you are doing. The help you receive from them is more emotional than anything else. They are there to encourage you, remind you of how special you are, and be a shoulder to lean on whenever you need to vent or cry.

The second type is your vendors. These people also do not work directly for you, but you need them in order to do what you do. They may be your supplier, accountant, lawyer, contractors, real estate agent, proprietor, etc. They are there to help you make good business decisions and to collaborate with you so that you all make a profit. Finally, the third type is your employees. They do work for you and are there specifically to do the things you need in order to fulfill your goals.

As you can see, your entourage can easily become a large number of people. However, big dreams require many people. If you take a good look at any successful corporation, you find many employees, vendors, and family and friends involved in making it all possible. Ask God to help you create an entourage full of people who really have your best interests in mind and believe in the vision. Nehemiah needed a crew and so do you.

# PRAYER

*Father, I know that I am only one person and that it takes many people to bring to past this great vision You have placed inside of me. Lead me to the right people who can build this thing with me. Show me what family and friends I can depend on for support. Bring to me vendors that will be a blessing to my business. Give me discernment over which employees to hire that can walk with me towards fulfilling this dream. Direct me as I create this team and counsel me on who to use and where to position them. I pray for these things in the name of Jesus. Amen*

# EXPECT OPPOSITION

Reading: Nehemiah 4

**When Sanballat heard that we were rebuilding the wall, he became angry and was greatly incensed. He ridiculed the Jews... But when Sanballat, Tobiah, the Arabs, the Ammonites, and the men of Ashdod heard that the repairs to Jerusalem's walls had gone ahead and that the gaps were being closed, they were very angry. They all plotted together to come and fight against Jerusalem and stir up trouble against it. But we prayed to our God and posted a guard day and night to meet this threat.**
**Nehemiah 4:1-9 (NIV)**

Anytime you are doing the right thing you will provoke opposition. Your adversary seeks to kill, steal, and destroy everything good in you. He will set all types of tricks and traps for you and will use anyone against you. The most foolish thing you can do is be unprepared for his resistance.

The question is not if we will experience conflict, but when and where it will arise. We make ourselves vulnerable to the antagonist when we expect only smooth and clear sailing with no unexpected winds. When difficulty comes, we are caught off guard and left feeling surprised and disappointed that things did not go as we'd wanted. Our lack of readiness is sometimes so severe that one hard blow and we are out for the count; ready to give up and give in.

Nehemiah and his crew faced the opposition of others as they attempted to rebuild the walls and gates of Jerusalem. It started with one group of people teasing them and escalated to several groups of people plotting war against them. If they had not been prepared to handle these challenges, it could have really hindered their progress. Can you imagine the emotions that would have arisen if they had not expected resistance? Workers probably would have become afraid and walked off the job feeling it wasn't worth the fight. However, because they were well organized and anticipated the barriers, they easily put their back-up plan into effect.

What is your emergency plan? How do you plan to handle conflict? Nehemiah dealt with his enemies by praying and placing a guard on duty. He reacts to the problem on both spiritual and natural levels. His spiritual response of prayer led him to respond naturally with a 24/7 guard. As you experience opposition, your first reaction should be to pray. Your talks with God will cause you to make wise physical decisions on how to handle the situation.

Be prepared for challenges as you begin and grow your business. If Jesus faced conflict in his mission to redeem us, why wouldn't you also experience barriers on the road to glorifying Him? Expect opposition and–if possible–have a back-up plan in place so that when it comes, it will not stop your progress.

## PRAYER

*Alpha and Omega, You know my beginning and my end. You know what struggles I will face before I experience them. I ask that You help me to be ready for all the plans of the wicked that would attempt to stop the good work You are doing in and through me. Be close, Lord, so that I can seek Your face on at the first sign of trouble. Keep me in perfect peace as challenges threaten my business and me. Give me the wisdom to know what I must do in the flesh to overcome these obstacles. Thank you in advance for your protection. In the name of Jesus. Amen.*

# ALL I HAVE

Reading: Luke 21:1-4

**As he looked up, Jesus saw the rich putting their gifts into the temple treasury. He also saw a poor widow put in two very small copper coins. "I tell you the truth," he said, "this poor widow has put in more than all the others. All these people gave their gifts out of their wealth; but she out of her poverty put in all she had to live on."**
**Luke 21:1-4 (NIV)**

Sacrifice is about giving out of your lack and not out of your wealth. The story in Luke explains this concept to us. The widow's two coins are more valuable than all the money that the rich gave combined because it was all she had. Jesus is more impressed with quality and not quantity, more excited about the sacrifice than the actual giving.

What pleases you more? Are you a quantity or quality person? Are you more impressed by the employee that wakes up at five in the morning to catch two buses to get to the job on time or by the employee that gets to work thirty minutes early driving his brand new luxury car? Would you prefer the customer who faithfully comes into your store weekly to buy $50 of needed products or the one that comes in one time only and nonchalantly spends $500?

There is something to be said about those who sacrificially give. Faith is at the root of giving what one does not have to give. When we come to Jesus, He expects us to come in a sacrificial manner, bringing all we have to Him. Our life becomes a constant living sacrifice as we surrender our every hope, desire, and thought to Him.

If your business plans are really about Jesus and fulfilling what He has placed within you, as time goes by you will witness yourself giving all you have, however, it will no longer be about you. That dream you always had will become a vehicle for blessing someone else; the vision will come to have kingdom purposes.

Do not be afraid to give the Lord all you have. He will return your faith with so much more. As you let go of the things that seem so important, you make room for the things that are truly worth value, such as a closer walk with the Father. Many times God will put you in situations that require you to give out of your lack just to see if you have enough faith and love for Him to come completely to Him, holding nothing back. Are you fully committed to Him and His purpose? Can you trust Him with everything? Are you truly ready to offer all you have?

## PRAYER

*Jesus, You came to earth and gave all that You had. Let me follow Your example and be someone willing to give all of me. It is so easy for me to give what is convenient for me, but if I truly trust You with my life, I should be able to surrender so much more. I give You my business plans and all my desires for self-employment. Let this business be about You and the fulfillment of Your will. I commit my life to You. In the name of Jesus Christ. Amen.*

# REACHING OUT

Reading: Matthew 7

**Ask and it will be given to you; seek and you will find; knock and the door will be opened to you. For everyone who asks receives; he who seeks finds; and to him who knocks, the door will be opened.**
**Matthew 7:7-8 (NIV)**

In order to receive the things that we need, we must be willing to reach out beyond ourselves. Independence and self-sufficiency can be harmful traits in our mission to know God and obtain his blessings. In our relationship with God, we must learn to be dependent and reliant, two words that this world abhors.

In this passage, Jesus ministers to the people and tells them that they must reach out for help. If there is something they want or need they must first ask for it; if there is something they want to find they must start with looking for it; if there is a door or opportunity they need opened, they must begin with knocking. It appears common sense, but it is not.

How many of us are unwilling to look beyond ourselves and what we can do for ourselves for assistance? How many of us would allow our pride to hold us hostage from the things we need because we do not want to ask, seek, or knock? Our society teaches us that to be independent is where all the glory resides. "I can do it all by myself. I don't depend on anyone! The only people I need are me, myself, and I." These statements are self-centered and opposing to the truth of God.

God created you to be dependent and connected to Him. Your business should be an extension of the body of Christ. You do not go into business for yourself to be independent; you do it to be even more connected. By becoming an entrepreneur, you allow yourself to rely even more on God and on other people to help you succeed.

Ambitious people are known for being too independent. Because God has given us so many strengths and talents, we unconsciously become self-reliant and overly dependent on ourselves. We forget that we are nothing without God and in fact, it is really Him in us allowing us to do as much as we do. Hard times, tragedies, and failures bring us back to the reality that Christ is the key to all that we are.

No matter what the world tells you, reach out for the blessings of the Lord. Reach out for help from others. Reach out to be connected to the body of Christ. Whatever you need or are looking for, God has it. Reach out and ask, seek, knock.

## PRAYER

*Messiah, I need You today in order to be all that I am. You are the source of life in me that allows me to do the impossible. Without You, I am nothing. I admit that at times I have leaned too much on myself and not enough on You. Forgive me for believing the deceit of independence. For the things I need in my life, I reach out to You Lord. I ask, seek, and knock, trusting that You hear me and that Your response will be to give, find, and open doors. In Jesus' name, I pray. Amen.*

# NEED A VACATION?

Reading: Matthew 11:25-30

**"Come to me, all you who are weary and burdened, and I will give you rest. Take my yoke upon you and learn from me, for I am gentle and humble in heart, and you will find rest for you souls. For my yoke is easy and my burden is light."**
**Matthew 11:28-30 (NIV)**

Entrepreneurs work harder than regular employees without the benefit of paid vacation time. When everyone else has gone home for the night, we are still there planning, calculating, and figuring things out. When all are snuggled up in their beds, enjoying a peaceful night's sleep, we are tossing and turning, creating new ideas or solving old problems. There are no weekends, no holidays, and no paid time off for business owners.

After a while, working so hard and carrying such a heavy load wears us down. Our minds start to play tricks on us because they are so exhausted; our bodies refuse to cooperate with us. We begin to feel like a Mac truck has hit us. We are desperately in need of a break; but with no money or time to get away how can we revive ourselves?

The R & R we need is in Christ. He stands in front of us with outstretched arms, welcoming us to Him for the break we require to keep going. In the Bible, Jesus promises that we can receive rest in Him when we feel weary and burdened. What great news!

Even ambitions people need to take a vacation from time to time. God, who is the most excellent of us all, even rested. He made everything in six days and on the seventh, He rested. If God took a break, why do we think that we can go without one?

There are several ways to get a much-needed vacation without breaking the bank or spending too much time away from your business. You can use the Sabbath for what it was originally meant for, a day to rest. You can have what a friend and I call a "Bum Day." Pick a day, any day, and for the whole day do not do anything productive. Don't get dressed, don't take a shower, don't even answer the phone. Just lay around as if you don't have a responsibility in the world. When the day is over return back to the clean and responsible person that you normally are. Other ideas for rest is to get a hotel room somewhere in your city where you can get away, go somewhere local like a park or museum that allows your mind to wonder, curl up with a good book that has nothing to do with your business or other worries, or simply have a night on the town with a couple of your closest friends.

For someone who has a lot to do, it is very hard to take a whole day and not do anything, but in order for us to be our best, we have to get enough rest. Spiritually, at any time we can come to God and get the vacation that we need for our souls. When you need peace and joy, the Lord is a close as a prayer, but you have to make the first move. Never hesitate to get the break your mind, body, and soul crave.

## PRAYER

*Jesus, You promise to give me rest for my weary soul. I have been faithful to the vision You have entrusted me with, but sometimes I feel beat down, broke down, and down and out. I come to You now for the spiritual, mental, and physical vacation that I desperately need. Soothe my fatigue with Your peace, joy, and tranquility. Take my heavy burden and replace it with Your light and easy yoke. Thank You for rest and revival. In the name of Jesus. Amen.*

# I SURRENDER ALL

Reading: Luke 14

**If anyone comes to me and does not hate his father
and mother, his wife and children, his brothers and
sisters – yes, even his own life – he cannot be my
disciple. And anyone who does not carry his cross and
follow me cannot be my disciple...In the same way,
any of you who does not give up everything he has
cannot be my disciple.**
**Luke 14:26-27, 33 (NIV)**

Walking with Jesus includes giving up everything that has
value to you. It is not that you cannot have wonderful people
and beautiful things in your life, but those people and things
cannot interfere in your obligation to Christ. He comes first
and is most important. Everything else must be placed in its
proper perspective.

At times, you will find God testing you, revealing to you
where your commitment truly lies. He will take something
you hold dear and place it on an alter as He did with Abraham
and Isaac. He will ask you to sacrifice someone or some item
that has a great significance to you. It will be your willingness
to let that person or thing go that will reflect your loyalty and
faith to Christ.

In this text, Jesus tells the people that in order to be a
disciple of His they must be willing to hate everyone including
their own self, give up everything, and take up their crosses.
He is basically saying to them that nothing should matter, but
following Him. When you get to a place where nothing at all
matters, but God, where you are willing to let go of all that the
world thinks is important, you are now ready to have
everything. You cannot handle having everything unless it
does not mean much to you. If you care too much for things

then you will find yourself struggling with loving people and things more than you love God.

As you pursue business success, realize that God may ask you to give up everything. You are asking God for it all, money, power, and respect, so God will have to make sure He can trust you with so much before He can grant your request. If you can sincerely submit everything to Him, He can then endow you with so much more.

God wants us to have fulfillment in life, but not if it will risk our purpose in Him. Just as a parent will not allow a child to have certain privileges that they are not ready for, neither will God. He does us a huge favor by keeping things from us that would ruin us.

Can you let go of everything for the sake of following Christ? Can you trust Him with the most prized possessions of you life? Is He truly first and most important to you? Be real with yourself as you answer these questions. If you want to be His disciple, letting go is the first step.

## PRAYER

*Jesus, I surrender all to You. I give You everything that is of value to me. I place in Your control: my life, my family, my friends, my home, my cars, my finances, my business, everything. I want to be Your disciple. I want to take up my cross and follow You. Nothing matters more to me than being close to You. These worldly things are temporary, but you are eternal. Thank you for the freedom You give from being attached to this world. In Your name, Christ Jesus. Amen.*

# EXPOSING YOUR WEAKNESS

Reading: 1 Samuel 1

**Whenever the day came for Elkanah to sacrifice, he would give portions of the meat to his wife Peninnah and to all her sons and daughters. But to Hannah he gave a double portion because he loved her, and the Lord had closed her womb. And because the Lord had closed her womb, her rival kept provoking her in order to irritate her. This went on year after year. Whenever Hannah went up to the house of the Lord, her rival provoked her till she wept and would not eat. Elkanah her husband would say to her, "Why are you downhearted? Don't I mean more to you than ten sons?"**
**1 Samuel 1:4-8 (NIV)**

The enemy watches us closely. There is no confusion regarding why he is called the father of lies. The bible refers to him walking back in forth throughout the world, seeking whom he can devour (1 Peter 5:8). He knows your weaknesses. The things that tempt you, the things that you lack, the things that would cause you to stumble, he knows. Sooner or later, he will attempt to imprison you through your weakness.

Hannah wanted a child. It was her weakness. If you have ever met a barren woman, you may have an idea of the heartache she was experiencing. Her husband's other wife, Peninnah, could bear him children and would use this against her. She would tease and mock her to the point where Hannah was so depressed that she would cry and could not eat.

Have you ever felt this way? Has there ever been something you wanted or needed so badly that it became your weakness? Is there a resource or information that your business requires so much that it has become the area of vulnerability within your company?

Like Peninnah, the enemy will identify our weaknesses and use them to keep us tied up and tangled up in depression and self-pity. He will remind us how broke we are, how no one else believes except us, how much we don't know, and of the risk of failing. We may respond, like Hannah, refusing to eat and finding ourselves in tears as we deal with the reality of our circumstances.

What Peninnah did not know was that as she provoked her rival, she was pushing Hannah to the throne of God. Hannah ended up taking her problem to God with so much intensity that the man of God thought she was drunk. In the end, she conceived a son named Samuel who became a major player in the Old Testament.

As the enemy aggravates you with the details of your natural life and lies about the future of your business, realize he may be doing you a favor. The more he pushes you into despair, the more he may be pushing you to reach out in desperation to the Lord. Your breakthrough is not in arguing with your foe, it is in retaliating by going to the Master and letting God make your weakness your strength. The Father is ready and able to turn your mourning into dancing. Hannah's answered prayer was Samuel, what will yours be?

## PRAYER

*Father God, You are aware of the internal pain and struggle that I feel. You know about my tearful nights and dispirited days. You even know about the times I couldn't eat because I was so heartbroken and anxious about the state of my business. The enemy wants to destroy me and the vision that You've placed with me. But I come to You with the faith that what I cannot do, You are able. What I cannot make come to past, You can. Change my situation; turn my weakness into my strength, birth a Samuel in my business, Lord. Thank you, Father, for Your delivering power. In Jesus' name. Amen.*

# DON'T BE AFRAID

Reading: Matthew 14:22-36

**But Jesus immediately said to them: "Take courage! It is I. Don't be afraid." "Lord, if it is you," Peter replied, "tell me to come to you on the water." "Come," he said. Then Peter got down out of the boat, walked on the water and came toward Jesus. But when he saw the wind, he was afraid and, beginning to sink, cried out, "Lord, save me!" Immediately Jesus reached out his hand and caught him. "You of little faith," he said, "why did you doubt?"**
**Matthew 14:27-31 (NIV)**

Fear, in my opinion, is the biggest reason most people never become all that they could be. It is so easy to allow fear to take over and when it does, your dreams and plans vanish. Fear is the opposite of faith and faith is the key ingredient to watching your vision come to life.

In the biblical story of Peter walking on water, both fear and faith are expressed. Peter begins in a state of faith, telling Jesus to call him out onto the water, but once out on the water, finds himself struggling with fear when he sees the wind. Luckily for Peter, Jesus was there to save him.

Our pursuit of entrepreneurship can at times mirror the experience of Peter. At first, we see the vision and believe God can bring it to past. We move out on faith, leaving our jobs, advertising our businesses, investing our time and money into our dreams. Initially, everything is great. We are walking on water. We are watching the miracle take place. Our faith is complete. Then the wind comes. The wind represents anything that takes our eyes off Jesus or that instills fear in us.

Instead of remaining in faith, we allow the wind to embed anxiety within us. And like Peter, we begin to sink.

Our businesses begin to suffer. We experience financial crisis. We lose customers. It seems as if failure is certain. Nevertheless, all hope is not lost. The cause and the cure are the same. We are sinking because we lost faith and it will take that same faith to save us.

If you are experiencing the sinking of your business, honestly assess your level of faith. Ask yourself, when you let the wind steal your faith? If you are still walking on water, remind yourself daily to put your trust the Lord and not your situation. Don't allow fear to drown everything you've worked so hard for. Don't be afraid.

## PRAYER

*Thank you, Jesus, for giving me the faith to step out into this business endeavor. I know that if I believe and do not doubt miracles will occur in the life of my business. However, I also know that if I allow fear to take over, I risk the survival of my business. Please show me how to retain my faith no matter how hard the wind blows. Help me to keep my eyes focused on You. In Jesus name, I pray. Amen.*

# MINIMIZE DISTRACTIONS

Reading: 2 Samuel 11 & 12

**One evening David got up from his bed and walked around on the roof of his palace. While he was on the roof he saw a woman bathing. She was very beautiful. So David sent his servants to find out who she was. A servant answered, "That woman is Bathsheba daughter of Eliam. She is the wife of Uriah the Hittite." So David sent messengers to bring Bathsheba to him. When she came to him, he had sexual relations with her.**
**2 Samuel 11:2-4 (NCV)**

King David was in the middle of a war when he allowed himself to be caught up in one of the biggest scandals of the bible. He was minding his own business when he saw a beautiful, naked woman. Unable to resist the temptation, he had her brought to him even though he knew she was married and her husband was fighting in the war. He engaged in sex with her and she became pregnant. Instead of admitting his sin, he attempted to cover it up by trying to trick the husband of the woman to have sex with her so that it could seem like the woman was really pregnant by her husband. However, the husband was so dedicated to the war that he refused to go home. When David's plan A didn't work, he moved onto plan B, which was a conspiracy to have the husband killed during the war. Once the husband died, David married Bathsheba, but the story doesn't end there. Because of David's sin, the child became very sick and died. David experienced not only a loss of focus, but also a whirlwind of drama, stress, and pain, because he allowed himself to get distracted.

Anytime you are doing something important, distractions will come. It is inevitable. Distractions range in size and intensity. You may have small or little distractions such as a phone call or an unexpected visitor or you may have larger and bigger distractions such as an emergency or a crisis situation. Distractions have one goal: to remove your focus from your priority long enough to stop your progress by drawing attention to some irrelevant, unproductive, and sometimes destructive matter.

Your vision is sacred and your business is your natural effort to fulfill the will of God. Life will not stop so that you can reach your dreams. The world will not pause so that you can complete your assignment. The enemy will not go away so that you can magnify the Lord. Distractions will come on a daily basis to do what they do–divert. You cannot avoid them, but you can minimize them. Be proactive. Preconceive what will come and set up methods to handle distractions before they appear. Turn off the ringer, hire an on call babysitter, keep the take-out food restaurant on speed dial, have a computer and a laptop, know where the local library is and have a library card, etc. If you, like David, find temptation knocking at your door, drop to your knees immediately and pray for strength. The word tells us that we can resist the enemy, and if we do, he will leave us (James 4:7).

Don't allow the issues of this world to keep you from completing the mission that God has entrusted to you. People need your gift, your talent, your business, your ministry. Minimize distractions and you will accomplish the Lord's purpose in your life.

## PRAYER

*Lord, I desire to let You finish the good thing that You have begun in me. Help me to avoid getting caught-up in distractions. Show me how to minimize distractions by being prepared for the things that would remove my focus from my goals. Strengthen me so that I can resist temptation. Show me the consequences of unproductive behavior in advance so that I am not fooled or deceived into destructive decisions. Be my guiding light and my defense against the issues of life. In Jesus' name. Amen.*

# VULNERABLE

Reading: Luke 4:1-14

**Jesus, filled with the Holy Spirit, returned from the Jordan River. The Spirit led Jesus into the desert where the devil tempted Jesus for forty days. Jesus ate nothing during that time, and when those days were ended, he was very hungry. The devil said to Jesus, "If you are the Son of God, tell this rock to become bread." Jesus answered, "It is written in the Scriptures: A person does not live by eating only bread."**

**Luke 4:1-4**

There are certain times in our lives when we are more vulnerable than usual. Typically, during times of transition and preparation, we find ourselves susceptible to the misleading and deceit of the enemy. In these moments, we must be watchful and careful that we do not fall prey to the temptations of sin and evil.

In these verses in Luke, Jesus is experiencing a time of transition. Up until this point in the bible He has been discussed as it relates to his childhood and developmental stages. Now as an adult, He moves into His position of leadership. In the midst of His transition into ministry, He spends over a month in isolation. While alone, He fasts from food and is repeatedly tempted by the devil. Although His natural body is weak, spiritually He remains strong and is able to resist the tactics of the enemy.

If the devil would challenge Jesus in these ways, why wouldn't he come to us in the same manner? Why wouldn't he purposely wait until we found ourselves in a moment of physical, spiritual, emotional, or mental weakness and then come to us offering the world on a silver platter? Why wouldn't he get us alone or in an isolated position and attempt to deceive us with trickery and mental games? The truth is that he would and he does.

Over two-thousand years later, his tactics are the same: exploit vulnerabilities. Expect to see the enemy show up, enticing you towards the very things you lack, need, and deeply desire. Food if you're hungry, love if you're lonely, wealth if you're broke, and power if your nobody.

Especially as you seek success in entrepreneurship, be on alert to his tempting methods. You long for your business to grow and mature and he is very aware of this. He will strategically set traps to catch you in his web of deceit. Your two greatest defenses are knowing God and knowing the enemy. Allow your constant conversation with God to direct you in all your ways. Ask Him to reveal truth to you every day and in every way. At the same time, remember who the enemy is and how good he is at his job. Keep in mind that he will not come looking like the devil he is, but instead he will appear as an angel of light.

When you are experiencing changing times and situations, be prepared for malicious plots. Be skeptical and prayerful, bringing all things to the Lord. Let God's light shine upon every thought and plan, revealing its underlying truth. Don't allow your vulnerability to cause you to stumble.

## PRAYER

*Holy Spirit, fill me like You filled Jesus and help me to resist the temptations of the enemy. During times of transition, I am more vulnerable to the attacks of the devil. I need Your strength and power to stand without wavering. I need Your wisdom and truth to see every trap the enemy has laid before me. I bind every trick, temptation, and evil plot in the name of Jesus. With Your guidance, Holy Spirit, I will not be fooled. Amen.*

# THE PROCESS

Reading: Matthew 25

**"After a long time the master came home and asked the servants what they did with his money. The servant who was given five bags of gold brought five more bags to the master and said, 'Master, you trusted me to care for five bags of gold, so I used your five bags to earn five more.' The master answered, 'You did well. You are a good and loyal servant. Because you were loyal with small things, I will let you care for much greater things. Come and share my joy with me.'"**

**Matthew 15:19-21 (NCV)**

In this biblical parable told by Jesus, a master goes out of town and entrusts three of his servants with different amounts of money. When he comes back he asks the three what they did with his money. Two of the three used the money to make more money, but one servant hid the money and did not use it to make more. The two who made more money, the master was pleased with and gave them more. However, the master punished the one who did not make more money by taking away what he had and giving it to the one with the most money.

God expects us to use what He gives us, no matter how little or how great it is. For this life on earth, God gives us authentic gifts and talents. He desires that we utilize every gift and talent we are blessed with. Some of us are only entrusted with one talent. It may be to sing, draw, play a sport, or preach. Whatever it is, there is something in which we excel. To others of us, He gives multiple talents. We may have two or three things we are really good at. And then there are us that have many talents. We might have six or seven various abilities that come naturally. No matter how many gifts we are given, we owe it to the Lord to be faithful to all of them and use them as tools to serve Him.

Until we learn to use and be a good steward over the few things he has given us, He will not allow us to have even more. Yet if we show God that we can be trusted by using what He has naturally given us, then we become applicable for even more. That's the process. In order to have more we must prove ourselves worthy. Many of us complain about not having all that we feel we should have, but we haven't even begun to take advantage of what is already within us.

What gifts has the Lord given you? How many talents do you have? Have you found ways to make money or serve God using what you already have? Is your business based in one of the unique gifts the Lord has placed in you? Are there other skills you have that have been unused or overlooked?

Everything you need to be successful is inside of you. God instills in each of us exactly what we need to be prosperous; we just refuse to take advantage of what we have. We are like the servant that hides the money given to him. Do we really think God will be pleased with us if we sit on the very things He gave us to use?

Develop the gifts and talents within you. Use your business to build on the various skills that come naturally to you. Find ways to serve the Lord with all of the things that make you special. If you do, God will be pleased and bless you by giving you even more.

## PRAYER

*Father, You have instilled inside of me so many special and unique qualities and characteristics. I admit that I have not always taken advantage of the wonderful gifts that I possess. If I would have, I would be further along in this life. Forgive me for hiding my treasures. Help me to find ways to serve You using these awesome talents. Assist me in making money by exploiting these traits. Show me how to build the kingdom by offering my skills. Thank You, Lord for your everlasting love that gives me a second chance to get it right. In the name of Jesus. Amen.*

# ARE YOU WILLING TO LEAVE YOUR COMFORT ZONE?

Reading: Exodus 2-4

**Moses went back to Jethro, his father-in-law, and said to him, "Let me go back to my people on Egypt. I want to see if they are still alive." Jethro said to Moses, "Go, I wish you well." While Moses was still in Midian, the Lord said to him, "Go back to Egypt, because the men who wanted to kill you are dead now." So Moses took his wife and his sons, put them on a donkey and started back to Egypt. He took with him the walking stick of God.**
**Exodus 4:18-20 (NCV)**

After Moses fled from Egypt, he began a new life in Midian. He met a woman, got married, and even had a few children. Life seemed to be going pretty well for him until God called him to return to Egypt to set God's people free. Life had finally become comfortable for Moses, and now he had to get up and leave.

Can you relate to Moses' situation? Have you finally gotten to a place in your life where things are running smoothly, the bills are paid, purchased a nice house, a brand new car, maybe even started a family and now God tells you to do something risky? I've been there. When I received the assignment to start my business I had just bought a home and new car one year prior, finally gotten my credit back on track, and was even starting to enjoy traveling again. Right in the middle of my parade, God shows up pointing me in a brand new direction. Not only was it going to be something new, but I knew it would also be extremely uncomfortable. I knew I'd be risking everything that I had worked so hard to build over the last few years. What is a faithful woman to do, but take a deep breath, get on my donkey, and start back to Egypt?

When you are called to be an entrepreneur, you must accept that life can no longer be comfortable. All the luxuries that your friends and family enjoy, you may not be able to. When everyone else is out shopping, buying Christmas gifts, going out to dinner, vacationing, spending money here and there, you have to live modestly. When everyone is relaxing at the end of the workday, you need to stay up late to finish a long to-do list. When other's weekends and holidays are free, yours are spent chained to your desk or to some project that has to be completed. Most people are not equipped for entrepreneurship because they are unwilling to be uncomfortable.

If you are considering starting a business, ask yourself these questions: Are you willing to leave your comfort zone? Are you willing to risk it all for the vision you see every time you close your eyes? Can you handle the loss that comes with gain? If you already own a business, ask yourself this question: Can you continue living in a state of discomfort?

If you cannot handle discomfort, business ownership is not for you. Nothing great is achieved overnight. Most successful business people are where they are because of years of dedication, sacrifice, and discomfort. However, don't get discouraged. Although the road is rough, ask any entrepreneur and most will tell you, it's worth it.

## PRAYER

*Almighty God, following You is not always easy and will at times cause me discomfort. God, I am willing to leave what is predictable and familiar to pursue this vision You have placed within me. Give me the strength to stick to it when the stress feels unbearable and hard times make it seem like it is not worth it. I know if You are leading me into this thing that You will bring me through it. Thank You, Christ for Your gift of the Comforter that is always with me, helping me in the most difficult situations. In Jesus name, I pray. Amen.*

# RUN TO WIN

Reading: 1 Corinthians 9

**You know that in a race all the runners run, but only one gets the prize. So run to win! All those who compete in the games use self-control so they can win a crown. That crown is an earthly thing that last only a short time, but our crown will never be destroyed. So I do not run without a goal. I fight like a boxer who is hitting something-not just the air. I treat my body hard and make it my slave so that I myself will not be disqualified after I have preached to others.**
**1 Corinthians 9:24-27 (NCV)**

What are your goals? How bad to you want to accomplish them? Are you willing to exert self-control in order to be successful? Many of us want to experience the highs of achievement, but are not willing to submit ourselves to the lows of the race.

Paul advises us to not only run, but to run to win. What is the point of entering a race if you have no goal, no aim, no direction, and no desire to win? You are just taking up space and wasting time. There are others out there that really want to win and you are simply in the way.

Paul is speaking of wining in the race of life and receiving the crown of eternal life with the Lord, but these same principals can relate to our business lives. If we want to receive the status of having a long-term successful business, we have to be willing to work hard for it. We have to train, develop, and challenge ourselves. We cannot allow our flesh to become a hindrance to us.

I love how Paul discusses using self-control and making his body a slave. You truly are your own worst enemy. Your mind and body have the ability to keep you from everything you've ever wanted. In order to enjoy the taste of success, you will have to exert control over yourself. You will have to fight against sleep, fatigue, complaining, hunger, laziness, doubt, fear, frustration, disappointment, depression, illness, instant gratification, etc. Your mind and body will have to submit to the bigger picture: business success.

It is not an easy task getting yourself to cooperate with you. Especially if you've always spoiled yourself, allowing yourself to have everything you always wanted, now getting yourself to comply will come with resistance. However, if you don't give up and continue to retrain your mind and body, eventually they will join in the race, on your team.

How important is business success to you? How bad do you want to win? Prepare yourself to endure the lows so that you can enjoy the highs. Run to win or don't run at all.

## PRAYER

*As I run this race, Lord, my goal is to win. I plan to win everlasting life with You. I also aim to win in creating a long-term successful business. I know I will have to train. I accept I will have to take control over my mind and body. Assist me, God, in the challenge and help me become stronger, wiser, and better with time. I won't give up and I expect victory. Amen.*

# UNEXPECTED BLESSINGS

Reading: 1 Kings 17

**"You may drink from the stream, and I have commanded ravens to bring you food there." So Elijah did what the Lord said: he went to Kerith Ravine, east of the Jordan, and lived there. The birds brought Elijah bread and meat every morning and evening, and he drank water from the stream.**
**1 Kings 17:4-6 (NCV)**

As humans with our finite minds, we often limited the vast greatness of God. We put Him in a box, in which our brains can conceive, expecting Him to only do what we can rationalize. If we could ever learn to accept God for the boundless entity He really is, we would finally be able to experience a glimpse of the awesome God He truly is.

The Lord implemented a season of drought on the land. Despite this environmental situation, God takes care of Elijah. He directs Elijah to go to a certain place to live. There Elijah is able to drink from the stream and is fed twice daily by birds. If God could use birds to bring food to Elijah, then how much more could He do for us?

We worry about God's ability to take care of us and meet our needs. We are anxious about how bills will be paid, how and what we will eat, and what we will wear. But God does not fret about those issues. He knows who He is and what we need. These issues though huge to us are minor to Him.

Can you image the amazement of receiving food two times a day from ravens? That's the unlimited might of the Lord. What if we trusted him to do these kinds of miracles in our lives? What if we stopped looking to paychecks, at the mailbox, to the lotto, and all the other things we lean on? What if we just allowed God to bring us everything we needed in miraculous ways? Random people walking up to us blessing us with groceries, squirrels and stray cats bringing us twenty dollar bills, dogs showing up at our door with a brand new outfit. I know it sounds crazy, but it's not impossible. God is God; He can do the supernatural in our lives if we just opened our minds to the wonders of the Lord.

So will you continue to put the Almighty in a box that agrees with your limited thinking or will you release yourself to the endless possibilities that exist? Would you like to see the glory of God in your life? Let go of your presumptions and watch the Lord bring unexpected blessing in unforeseen ways.

## PRAYER

*Forgive me Lord for my small-minded thoughts. I've repeatedly placed You in a box that suits my understanding. I desire to see the miraculous gifts that You give. I believe you can meet all my needs and that you don't have to do it in the ways I am accustomed to. I open myself today and allow You to do the supernatural in my life. Let nothing that You do surprise me, Father, because I release myself to believe You can do anything. Amen.*

# WHO YOU KNOW

Reading: 1 Kings 17

**"Don't worry," Elijah said to her. "Go home and cook your food as you have said. But first make a small loaf of bread from the flour you have, and bring it to me. Then cook something for yourself and your son. The Lord, the God of Israel, says, 'That jar of flour will never empty, and the jug will always have oil in it, until the day the Lord sends rain to the land.'"**
**1 Kings 17:13-14 (NCV)**

There is a commonly used adage, "Sometimes, it's not what you know, but who you know." The motto simply means that you can be smart, knowledgeable, and intelligent, but if you don't have the right connections, you still may not be able to achieve your objectives. Because of this idea, many people spend much of their time, energy, and money trying to get to know the right people.

In this biblical story in First Kings, we find this saying to be true for the widow. She finds herself with only enough food to make one more meal for her and her son. If you've ever experienced a lack of food and money, you know how desperate and depressed this woman must have felt. Being unable to take care of oneself is difficult, but add-on not being able to provide for a child, and she had to be crushed. In the midst of this dilemma, a man asks her to bring him some food. Many of us would have cursed him for asking us for food in the middle of our lack. She explains to the man of God that she only has enough for one more meal for her and her son. He responds to this by telling her to cook him something first, then to cook for her family and she will not go without until God ends the drought. In faith, she follows his instructions and is provided the miracle of endless flour and oil.

She is blessed not because of what she knows, but because of who she knows. Because she is connected to the man of God, she now can care for her family. If this man with the untimely request had not come along, she and her son may have starved.

We also do not have to go without. Despite what we have or don't have, regardless of what we know or don't know, we are connected to Someone who can help us achieve our objects: God. As you proceed toward the goal of business ownership, stay connected to the One who can "hook you up." The Lord is able to provide for you when it seems as though you cannot provide for yourself. Knowing Him is more valuable than knowing all of the most influential people on earth.

# PRAYER

*Most High God, You are the One I need to know. You have ways of taking care of me that I can't even conceive. I know that no matter where my lack lies, You are able to bless me with endless supply. Take care of my business and me. Knowing You is the difference between starving and succeeding. Thank You, Father for Your infinite influence in my life. In the name of Christ Jesus. Amen.*

# INTERCEDE FOR YOUR STAFF

Reading: 1 Kings 17

**Then he prayed to the Lord: "Lord my God, this widow is letting me stay in her house. Why have you done this terrible thing to her and caused her son to die?" Then Elijah lay on top of the boy three times. He prayed to the Lord, "Lord my God, let this boy live again!" The Lord answered Elijah's prayer: the boy began breathing again and was alive.**
**1 Kings 17:20-22 (NCV)**

When others are helping you to achieve your vision, you owe them more than a little food, money, and a few "thank yous." Their presence makes it possible for you to do what you love to do. Therefore, when they find themselves in difficult situations, they deserve your prayers and intercession.

Elijah was a guest in the widow's home when her son fell sick. The boy dies and the widow falls apart. The man of God is so moved by her pain that he takes the boy into a room and prays over him. He intercedes until God answers him and the boy comes back to life.

In Elijah's prayer, he reminds God that he is living in this woman's home. Because he is a guest, he cannot just sit by and allow the woman to be devastated when he knows he can help. He has a direct relationship with God and he uses this to relieve the widow's heartache.

We must be like Elijah and be willing to pray for the needs and hurts of our staff. If they are hurting, going through and miserable, how can they be of assistance to us? Not only that, but we should grow to care for them as they have cared for our vision and us. Out of mutual love, we should be drawn to intercede on their behalves.

Faith without works is dead. How can you tell your employees God is going to work it out for you if you haven't even prayed for them yourself? If you truly believe that the Lord can change their situation, get on your knees and pray for their deliverance.

We are called to be leaders and leadership consists of being an example. We want our staff to share in our vision so we must share in theirs. We must join in the fight with them over their lives. We can't be selfish about our relationship with God. The next time you see an employee who is committed to you struggling with a hardship, commit to them and intercede about their cause. Allow God to use you in their lives just as He is using them in yours.

## PRAYER

*Heavenly Father, I lift all of my employees and staff up to You. You know the various pains, hurts, struggles, and issues in their lives. You are the God of healing and deliverance. Use these circumstances to obtain glory and bring them closer to You. Touch their lives and create positive change. Use me to intercede for them and reveal to me how I can pray for them. Help me to be a living example of what faith in You produces. In Jesus' name. Amen.*

# ENJOY YOURSELF

Reading: Ecclesiastes 3

**Do people really gain anything from their work? I saw the hard work God has given people to do. God has given them a desire to know the future. He does everything just right on time, but people can never completely understand what he is doing. So I realize the best thing for them is to be happy and enjoy themselves as long as they live. God wants all people to eat and drink and be happy in their work, which are gifts from God.**
**Ecclesiastes 3:9-13 (NCV)**

Solomon was known for his great wisdom. In these verses, and out of his intellect, he tells us that God wants us to enjoy our lives and our work. Not that every day will be happy, but life is a gift from God and we should find pleasure in it.

He reminds us that although we want to know what is going to happen, God does not reveal this to us. Instead, God does what He wants to do when He wants to do it. We sit around stressing ourselves by trying to figure the Lord out when we will never fully comprehend the ways of God. Therefore, Solomon offers this solution: enjoy yourself.

What would life be like if we stopped worrying about how things are going to work out? What if we let go of knowing the future and just went with the flow? What if we just lived life to the fullest, trusting God to do what He said He would do? How much happier would we be? How much more satisfied would we be with our careers, family life, and ourselves?

Just because we work does not mean we have to be miserable. We can love what we do. That is the whole point of being an entrepreneur. Yes, we want more and better opportunities and yes, we want more control over of schedules, however, even more so we want to feel good about what we do and how we do it. I left the regular work world because I was tired of being tired. I didn't want to struggle anymore with getting up in the morning because I hated what I did. I didn't want to give only half of myself when I knew I should be giving so much more. I didn't want to dread Sundays because Monday meant returning to the daily grind. I no longer wanted the only workday that meant something to me to be payday. I needed and wanted to love working.

God wants the same for us. He wants us to be free from worries because we can depend on Him to be God. Once we finally accept that the position of God is already taken, we will be better off. As you continue to pursue your business goals, let go of trying to know the future and learn to embrace enjoying today. Today, you are an entrepreneur. Today, you love what you do. Today, God is taking care of you. Today is a gift so enjoy yourself!

## PRAYER

*I praise You Most High, for this gift of life. You've given me another day and another chance to live to the fullest. I let go of every attempt to know the future and understand Your ways. I'll never completely comprehend what You are doing so I leave the future in Your hands. You are God and I trust You. I thank You for this business and the joy of loving what I do. Today, I aim to enjoy myself as I reflect on how great You are. In the name of Jesus. Amen.*

# JUST A TIME AS THIS

Reading: Esther 4

**Then Mordecai sent back word to Esther: "Just because you live in the king's palace, don't think that out of all the Jewish people you alone will escape. If you keep quiet at this time, someone else will help and save the Jewish people, but you and your father's family will all die. And who knows, you may have been chosen queen for just a time as this."**
**Esther 4:13-14 (NCV)**

What are you currently being challenged to do? What is at stake? Is there something that you have been put in a selected position to do? Do you think that you are where you are by chance, or is it possible that you've been placed in your situation for just a time as this?

Esther was strategically positioned by God as queen at a certain moment in time because she would be the deliverance the Jews needed. One of the king's right hand men were plotting to destroy the Jews. If it wasn't for Esther's bravery and her relationship with the king, the Jews may have experienced mass genocide.

Maybe you too are called for just a time as this. Your business might be the salvation someone needs; your company may be the deliverance a community requires. Will you turn your back on the people because there is too much to risk? Will you allow selfishness or fear keep you from doing the great thing God has put you in position to do? The most remembered and honored people in the world are those who didn't cower in the face of adversity. People like Martin Luther King Jr., John F. Kennedy, Rosa Parks, Apostle Paul, King David, Moses, and Jesus, will be continually honored because of their willingness to accept the call.

The people who excel in this world are those who take full advantage of the opportunities they are confronted with. Success is more than just being good; it's being at the right place at the right time. If MLK were born fifty years early or fifty years later, he would not be remembered for being a heroic civil rights leader. Moreover, if you weren't born when you were, experienced the things you have been through, and located where you are right now, you couldn't do the magnificent things you are destined to do.

Esther almost let her opportunity pass her by. Fear set in and Esther was tempted to walk away from her destiny. Mordecai warned Esther that if she didn't speak out not only would she lose her safety, but also someone else would do the job for her. How will you feel if you miss your time and another takes your place, doing all the things you were meant to accomplish? Esther took courage and stepped out in faith and you should too.

What opportunity awaits you? What is God's purpose in giving you this business? How can you make a difference? What is the need that you were chosen and strategically placed to fulfill? You are a business owner for just a time as this. Make a difference or someone else will.

## PRAYER

*Oh Great God, You've created me in Your image and bestowed upon me many magnificent blessings. Opportunities have presented themselves to me that are directly from You. I believe You've placed me strategically where I am for just a time as this. Help me not to be afraid of my adversary, but to take courage and move in faith. Touch others through my life and my business. Don't let another take my destiny or my dreams. I surrender my life to You, Lord. In the name of Jesus. Amen.*

# DELEGATING RESPONSIBILITY

Reading: Deuteronomy 1

**At that time I said, "I am not able to take care of you by myself. The Lord your God has made you grow in numbers so that there are as many of you as there are stars in the sky. I pray that the Lord, the God of your ancestors, will give you a thousand times more people and do all the wonderful things he promised. But I cannot take care of your problems, your troubles, and your arguments by myself. So choose some men from each tribe-wise men who have understanding and experience-and I will make them leaders over you.**
**Deuteronomy 1:9-13 (NCV)**

As much as we secretly believe we are supermen and superwomen, we are not. Over time, the mission God has given us can become too heavy for us to bear alone. Even Moses understood this concept. As the Lord continues to develop what he's given us, there will come a time when back-up is necessary.

Moses honestly assessed the magnitude of the job and concluded after struggling to handle it solely, "I can't do it by myself." How many of us need to come to this realization? The smartest leaders know the importance of delegating responsibility.

Delegating responsibility is the process of giving certain less important duties to others whom you trust so that you can be freed up to focus on ones that are more important. It's accepting that you can't be everywhere all the time. The children of Israel were arguing, fighting, and bickering about all sorts of things. They brought their problems to Moses because he was the man in charge. Eventually, it became too much. He couldn't focus on big issues because he was constantly dealing with little ones.

Moses handled the dilemma by telling the people to pick wise men from each tribe as their leaders. It is interesting that he didn't just say select of few people, but specified that they should be wise. As you choose people to help you run your business, it is important that you get the right people. Don't select managers just because of seniority or because they are family and friends. You need competent, intelligent, and knowledgeable people to be in key leadership positions. The wrong person in a high position is worse than having nobody in it at all.

As your business grows, don't be afraid to place various jobs in others' hands. Select people with the characteristics required to get the job done effectively. You don't have to carry the load alone, and more than likely, you can't do it anyway. Exhibit the wisdom to delegate responsibility and you will find yourself less stressed and more productive.

## PRAYER

*Messiah, I realize that I cannot do everything by myself. Even You walked the earth with twelve disciples and gave them jobs to do. Give me the wisdom to know what duties to entrust others with and exactly who is best for each task. Help me to get over the "super person" complex. As I let go of certain responsibilities allow me to be confident in my decisions, relax, and focus on the important roles that I have reserved for me to fulfill. In Christ's Name. Amen.*

# WRITE THE VISION

Reading: Habakkuk 2

**The Lord answered me: "Write the vision; write it clearly on tablets so whoever reads it can run to tell others. It is not yet time for the message to come true, but that time is coming soon; the message will come true. It may seem like a long tine, but be patient and wait for it, because it will surely come; it will not be delayed."**

**Habakkuk 2:2-3 (NCV)**

Whenever God gives you a vision, idea, dream, or goal, write it down. Writing it down accomplishes four things: 1) Helps you not to forget, 2) allows you to visualize the objective or concept, 3) becomes an affirmation of your future plans and, 4) communicates to others your strategy. If you fail to record your vision, you risk not fulfilling it due to having unclear goals.

In the world of entrepreneurship, a business plan is commonly created to assist leaders in starting their companies. This plan achieves the same four goals listed above. Not only does it demonstrate the feasibility of the project to the business owner, but it also helps other investors, partners, and employees understand the "big picture." Trying to get others involved and committed to your business requires that they believe in what you want to do. Establishing a business plan serves as a tool for communicating your vision to a second or third party.

Even if you do not have a formal business plan, you should create some form of written proposal for your business. It doesn't have to be perfect or specify every single detail of the business. You can add to it over time, so don't worry if you don't have all of the answers initially. However, you do want to jot down the parts of your vision that are certain for you and even some suggestions or possible ideas that you are still figuring out.

As you write out your plans you will began to feel more excited and confident in your dream. You will be able to review your progress and assess what still needs to be done. You can even check off little and big accomplishments as you make them. This will encourage you to keep moving forward when the road ahead seems so long and hard. Anytime I am working on a project I like to create these kinds of lists and strategic plans. Working on large assignments can easily become overwhelming. By breaking it down into little pieces and steps, a major job can begin to appear manageable.

If you are considering starting a business, write out a formal or informal business plan. If you already have a business, but don't have a plan, write down what you've already been doing and what you plan to do next. If you have a company and a business plan, go back to it periodically and revise it. Your business will change over the years and you want to keep up with changes and anticipate future goals and adjustments. Whatever stage you are currently at, it's time to write the vision. Make it plain and clear for the benefit of yourself and others.

# PRAYER

*Lord, I continue to praise You for the vision and ideas You've placed in my heart to accomplish. Because I have faith that these dreams will come to past, I take the time out today to write the vision and make it clear. As I sit down and write out my plans, guide me and give me wisdom on how to strategically map-out my business. Give me understanding on how to write a business plan. Show me the areas of my business that need to be revised and upgraded. Provide me with the knowledge to comprehend my industry and how my business can grow despite the economy and competition. Bless my business and the plan I am creating for it, Father. In Your Son, Jesus Christ's Name. Amen.*

# DON'T STOP!

Reading: Hebrews 6

**God is fair; he will not forget the work you did and the love you showed for him by helping his people. And he will remember that you are still helping them. We want each of you to go on with the same hard work all your lives so you will surely get what you hope for. We do not want you to become lazy. Be like those who through faith and patience will receive what God has promised.**
**Hebrews 6:10-12 (NCV)**

Stopping is a sure way to miss your goal. Even temporarily postponing your endeavor has the potential to lead to indefinite self-sabotage. The only way to guarantee your business and life objectives are met is to keep going.

Anytime you stop, you lose momentum. If you are driving fast then stop for a stop sign, getting your vehicle back to its former speed will take a little time and extra acceleration on the gas petal. The same truism exists in life. Stopping in the pursuit of your goal, will cause you to need more momentum to get going again.

Pursuing my doctoral degree was one of my most challenging undertakings. The hardest moments for me were at the start of a new semester. Once I finished a class or term, I would be hyped and eager. After every semester, there would be a small break for either a few days or a week, maybe two weeks. The brief pause between the old course and the new one would zap my energy. I always found myself struggling to get going again in the new class. It would usually take me until the third week of classes to build myself back up and get back in the game. This is a perfect example of how stopping, even briefly, can become a barrier to success.

If you are currently in the middle of chasing a dream, don't stop. Do something every day in a positive direction towards that goal. Even if it is a small, baby step, such as making a phone call, writing a letter, working on your business plan, looking for office space, buying office supplies, or filing business documents, you are still making progress. The worst thing you could do is to stop moving. Every day that you don't do something related to your business, you jeopardize your dreams ever coming true. So whatever you do, don't stop.

## PRAYER

*Dream Giver, You've entrusted me with this vision of entrepreneurship. You believe in me, which helps me to believe in myself. Give me the strength and the courage to continue down this path, no matter what may come. Help me to accomplish something related to my business every day. I don't want to lose momentum. I don't want to forsake my dreams. I promise not to give up or stop. If a day comes and goes and I have not completed a task towards business success, wake me up the next morning with urgency that I must move forward immediately. Thank You, Lord for never stopping Your pursuit of me. In the name of Jesus. Amen.*

# ARE YOU SATISFIED?

Reading: 2 Timothy 4

**My life has been given as an offering to God, and the time has come for me to leave this life. I have fought the good fight, I have finished the race, I have kept the faith.**

**2 Timothy 4:6-7 (NCV)**

One thing that concerns me most is how satisfied I will be at the end of my life. I would hate to spend many decades on this earth and in my final hours feel like I've wasted so much time. I don't want to have a bunch of regrets over the things that I could've and should've done, but didn't. So right now, while I still have life in me, I strive to be the best I can be.

Paul is nearing the end of his earthly journey when he writes this letter. In reviewing his life, he makes the conclusion that he is satisfied. He has fulfilled his purpose, he has done all that he could do, he has completed what he intended to accomplish. Imagine how much peace must have filled his soul to know that he "fought the good fight and kept the faith."

It is easy to let go of life when you've found satisfaction. Many people struggle with death because there is so much that is left undone. In their final hours, they try to make up for past mistakes and make amends to those they've hurt, but in most instances, it is too late.

So, how will you feel at the end of this life? Will you be able to say that you've fought the good fight, finished the race, and kept the faith? Will you have accomplished all that was set before you? Will you feel satisfied? Or, will you leave this life peace-less and filled with remorse and regret?

Now is the time for you to achieve all the wonderful things God has for you. The creation of your business is just the beginning of the greatness that the Lord wants to do in your life. There are so many ways that the Father wants to use you, but you must be willing to offer yourself completely and unrestrained.

Don't allow life to pass you by without being the best person you can be. Whatever desires, wants, needs, dreams, hopes, wishes, and interests you have, seek them out now. Push beyond your fears and reservations. Don't let insecurity, doubt, lack, or any other barrier stand in your way. Make a vow to yourself that you will be satisfied at the end of your journey. Promise yourself that you will make every minute count and reach for the stars every day of your life. Fight the good fight, keep the faith, and finish the race.

## PRAYER

*Most Holy God, You've given me this special gift called life. I regret that I have not always made the most of it. I have wasted some time and allowed opportunities to pass me by. But from this moment on, I vow to give myself as an offering to You. I promise to live every day to the fullest, completing every assignment You've given me. I will not live with remorse and could haves, should haves. Instead, I will push past obstacles and experience the joy of reaching for the stars. I will find peace in the end knowing that I have fought the good fight, kept the faith, and finished the race. In the name of Jesus. Amen.*

# HANDING OUT PROMOTIONS

Reading: Acts 1

**They put the names of the two men before the group. One was Joseph Barsabbas, who was called Justus. The other was Matthias. The apostles prayed, "Lord, you know the thoughts of everyone. Show us which one of these two you have chosen to do this work. Show us who should be an apostle in place of Judas, who turned away and went where he belongs. Then they used lots to choose between them, and the lots showed that Matthias was the one. So he became an apostle with the other eleven.**
**Acts 1:23-26 (NCV)**

As your business develops you will eventually get to a point where promoting someone is necessary. Either a current employee will leave, requiring you to fill their position, or you will need to appoint someone to do a newly created job or duty you can no longer do. Promoting someone, whether it is an inside or outside candidate, will be your next step. But how do you know whom to promote when you have more than one qualified applicant?

After Judas betrayed Jesus, there became an opening for the position of the twelfth apostle. Two men were selected as the top candidates, Justus and Matthias. Before the disciples chose which one would be promoted, they prayed and asked God to show them who was best for the job. Then they cast lots and the decision was made that Matthias should become the twelfth apostle.

As you are interviewing and assessing applicants for promotion or even hiring purposes, some of these same principles should be used to help you pick the right person. Three steps are taken by the apostles to ensure accuracy in their selection. First, they narrowed down their candidates to two people. It is too difficult to make a decision when you have too many options. Through your selection process, weed out applicants that do not have the qualifications that you are looking for, and narrow down your pool to the strongest two or three applicants. Second, they prayed. God knows the hearts of men and is able to reveal to us people's true motives. We cannot afford to make major decisions like handing out promotions without the guidance of the Lord. Seeking God's advice and direction should always be a priority in your hiring process. Finally, they conferred and made a decision collectively. Just because you are the owner or CEO doesn't mean that you shouldn't bring others into your interviewing process. People who work closely with you should be included in hiring and promotions. Many times employees feel resentful when there are new people hired or somebody is promoted because they have their reservations about the person based on things they know that you don't. By asking for input from other employees, you may gain information about your applicants that could help you make a wiser choice.

In my company, I try to use these steps to pick the best people. My employees are an extension my business and represent me at all times. If I choose the wrong person, not only do I end up wasting time and resources, but I also risk ruining my reputation and bringing unnecessary chaos into my work environment. When interviewing candidates, I sometimes include trusted employees in the actual interview or I discuss my thoughts and the responses of the interviewee with them later that day. I listen to their feedback and consider their comments as I am making decisions. In addition, during the interview I communicate to applicants the importance of building a family within my company and hiring people whose personality and professionalism mesh well with my existing staff. Before choosing whom I will hire, I ask myself, "Who will fit in the best with my staff? Will this person get along and blend in? What potential social issues could arise if I bring this person into my company?" These questions are important because the worst thing to have is work-related drama! Selecting the right people reduces needless and irrelevant hostility and disorder in your business.

Next time you must hire or hand out a promotion, keep the process used by the apostles in mind. Narrow down your candidates, pray for guidance, and choose collectively. Using these steps, you are more likely to pick the right person for the job.

## PRAYER

*Jehovah, I come to you for guidance and wisdom as I develop and build my business. There are jobs that I cannot do all by myself, so promotion and hiring is needed. Bring the right people to me during the times that I am hiring. Give me the discernment to know what people's true intentions are. Show me who would be best for the position based on professionalism, production, and personality. Guide me in which current employees to involve in the hiring process that can help me make the right choice. In addition, help us to select a good person who will build the company and not tear it down. I praise You for all that You are, and I thank You for your wisdom and knowledge. In the name of Jesus. Amen.*

# LET THEM TALK

Reading: 2 Samuel 16

**David also said to Abishai and all his officers, "My own son is trying to kill me! This man is a Benjaminite and has more right to kill me! Leave him alone, and let him curse me because the Lord has told him to do this. Maybe the Lord will see my misery ad repay me with something good for Shimei's curse today!"**
**2 Samuel 16:11 (NCV)**

You have to choose your battles wisely. Not every war is meant for you to fight. Sometimes and in some situations, the best thing you can do is walk away and let it go.

Walking away from something that is provoking you can be extremely hard to do. You may feel like handling the situation, going off, and even letting them know what is on your mind, but this is not always the best option. We will wear ourselves out trying to deal with every irritating problem that comes our way. Instead, saving our energy for more important issues can be a particularly wise decision.

David could have easily dealt harshly with Shimei and had every right to. Shimei was upset with David because he was a family member of Saul, the previous king. He felt David had killed Saul and his sons, so when he saw David, he began to yell at and curse him. David had his men with him and being annoyed by Shimei's blatant disrespect, could have simply said the word and had him killed or arrested. Nevertheless, he chose to let the man talk.

My pastor frequently asks the question, "If the Bible was written about you, what would it say?" Therefore, I pose the same question to you. If you were David, how would you have responded? How would verse eleven read? "Then David said bring him to me so that we may kill him?" Or how about, "Then David went off on him and cursed out his whole family?" However you would have handled the situation, most likely, "Leave him alone and let him curse me," would have not been the response.

As an entrepreneur, you will have people talking about you. They will say all sorts of negative things: talk about who you used to be, talk about what you aren't going to be, lie on you, tarnish your name, and curse you. You cannot allow yourself to be so sensitive. Bad talking comes with the territory. You must learn to trust God that He will protect your reputation and deal with those who seek to slander your name.

The next time someone tries to curse you out over foolishness, let them curse. When you find out someone is out to corrupt your name, let it go. If you witness someone bad talking you, let them talk. God is on your side and if He is for you, who can be against you (Romans 8:31)?

## PRAYER

*Heavenly Father, give me the strength and wisdom to be able to let things go. Show me which battles are mine to fight and which belong to You. Build me up so that I am no longer sensitive and easily angered. The road to greatness will not always be easy and people may not always like me. Help me to accept this and let people say what they want. Remind me that only what You say about me truly matters. Amen.*

# DO YOU REALLY TRUST GOD?

Reading: Genesis 22:1- 18

**After these things God tested Abraham's faith. God said to him, "Abraham!" And he answered, "Here I am." Then said, "Take your only son, Isaac, the son you love, and go to the land of Moriah. Kill him there and offer him as a whole burnt offering on one of the mountains I will tell you about."**
**- Genesis 22:1-2 (NCV)**

The true test of faith is when God asks you to give up or let go of the very things you cherish the most. Abraham watched the miracle come to past of his wife giving birth at an old age. Now, the very son that God had promised him, the very child that he had prayed for, was now the very sacrifice that the Lord requested. Could you imagine the confusion and heartache of Abraham? If it were one of us, would we have trusted God enough to let go?

As the story goes, Abraham did what God asked him and just before he went to kill the child, the Lord stopped him and provided an alternative sacrifice. I bet Abraham was relieved to find out he didn't have to give up his only son (from Sarah - his wife), but his willingness to trust God despite his own understanding led to God promising him that his family would be large and his descendants would be blessed.

From time to time, God will test our faith by asking us to sacrifice something we hold dear. In our businesses, He could ask us to give a sacrificial offering or let go of a needed resource such as a key employee or company site. The very thing that you praised God for and used as your testimony, could be the same thing He requests that you give up. If such a demand is made, what will you do? Will you argue with Him about it? Will you refuse to comply? Will you complain and grumble about it? Or, will you take on the attitude of Abraham and with a trusting heart, let go?

God does not need anything from us. He does not need our money, our business, or houses, our cars; there is nothing! He requests sacrifices from us to make sure we never become too bound to things of this world. As long as we are in love with worldly things, we cannot serve Him with our whole beings. How can we love Him with our whole heart, mind, body, and soul if we are constantly concerned with obtaining and keeping materialistic or temporal things?

If you really want to see the awesome blessings and favor of God in your business, be willing at a moment's notice to give something up. Be ready for God to ask you to let go of something special. When He comes, petitioning you for that beloved thing or person, trust Him. Remember: He is God, His ways are above ours, and without faith it is impossible to please Him.

## PRAYER

*Most awesome God, I come before You with praise upon my lips. You deserve all of the glory and honor for everything that is good in my life. I desire to love You the way You require, with my whole self. Let me be prepared to trust You and follow You at a moment's notice. Help me to remember that You know what is best for me. I place all that I have in Your hands and at Your disposal. In the soul saving name of Jesus, I pray. Amen.*

# FRIENDS, FAMILY, OR FOES?

Reading: Genesis 37

**Then Judah said to his brothers, "What will we gain if we kill our brother and hide his death? Let's sell him to these Ishmaelites. Then we will not be guilty of killing our own brother. After all, he is our own brother, our own flesh and blood." So when the Midianite traders came by, the brothers took Joseph out of the well and sold him to the Ishmaelites for eight ounces of silver. And the Ishmaelites took him to Egypt.**
**Genesis 37:26-28 (NCV)**

The people who intend to hurt you and the success of your business are not always on the outside, sometimes they are inside. Your friends and family could be the main people attempting to sabotage your endeavors. Using these people is a common trick of the enemy because he knows that these people can influence you so much more than anyone on the outside ever could.

These words of wisdom are not given to turn you against your family or make you paranoid by every action of your friends. They are to warn you not to be naïve to the schemes and devices of evil. The best ways to handle obstacles are to prepare for them in advance.

There are two types of inside people that can "sell you out" as Joseph's brother did to him. The first are people who really want to hurt you, but for the sake of their conscious, they rationalize it and attempt to do only "some" harm. They are jealous, envious, and malicious, but in their own way, they care about you. These people are like the brother Judah who convinces his other brothers to sell Joseph. In his mind, he doesn't think he is doing that much harm. He tells himself, "I could have killed him, but instead I just sold him into slavery." But honestly, is slavery really better?

The second type is like his other brother Reuben. Now Reuben wanted to save his brother, but instead of doing what was right and talking his brothers out of their plan or even telling his father the truth, he pretended to go along with the scheme then when things didn't go according to his plan, joined in with the lie the brothers told their father. Reuben probably told himself, "I tried to intervene, but it didn't work and now I can't tell my father the truth." These were Joseph's brothers–his family–and because they were threatened by the potential of his success, they allowed him to become a slave.

The very people who claim they love you will sometimes cause you the most pain. They will see you striving for something better, working hard to create and promote your business, and feel intimidated and threatened. They may attempt to bring you down with their words and actions, all the while rationalizing their behavior to themselves.

When you encounter these types of friends and family members, keep two things in mind. One, despite their actions, God always will bless you and take care of you. Joseph ends up being favored–even in slavery–and eventually becomes a leader in Egypt. Two, you don't have to allow people to mistreat or walk over you. If people are not in your life for good, you can with a gentle heart, love them from a distance.

Whether you have family members or friends like Judah or Reuben, both types of loved ones may sell you out. Pray to God for knowledge on how to handle these types of people. Don't let anyone's jealousy hinder you from your goals.

# PRAYER

*Jesus, You know how it feels to be betrayed by those who You loved. As I encounter friends and family that say they love me, but aim to block my goals, help me to have a forgiving heart. Empower me to deal with them gently and to return their evil with good. Show me if I need to distance myself from them and how I can do this without causing more strife. Be with me and bless me with Your favor no matter how they try to stop me. Turn all of their schemes against them and raise me up to be the leader You purposed me to be. In Your name, Jesus. Amen.*

# TOUGH DECISIONS

Reading: 1 Chronicles 21

**So Gad went to David and said to him, "This is what the Lord says: 'Choose for yourself three years of hunger. Or choose three months of running from your enemies as they chase you with their swords. Or choose three days of punishment from the Lord, in which a terrible disease will spread through the country. The angel of the Lord will go through Israel destroying the people.' Now, David, decide which of these things I should tell the Lord who sent me."**
**1 Chronicles 21:11-12 (NCV)**

The devil caused David to sin by tricking him into counting the people. As punishment for David's sin, God sent a messenger to give David a choice of what the consequence would be for his behavior. He was given these three choices: three years of hunger, three months of running from his enemies, or three days of disease among his kingdom. David chose the three days of disease and miserably watched as illness took the lives of 70,000 people. Seventy thousand people died because of David's sin, because of his bad decision.

As a business owner, you must always remember that a leader's actions affect everyone under his or her leadership. How you operate your business, the choices you make both good and bad, will have a trickle-down effect, impacting everyone who works for you. As we look at companies in the news that were surrounded in scandal, their leaders' illegal behaviors risked the jobs and reputations of every employee of the company.

How bad would you feel if 70,000 people died on your watch because of something you did wrong? How would you handle 200 people losing their livelihoods because you made a bad decision? Could you sleep at night if 50 or even 10 people who depended on you could no longer take care of their families because they are now unemployed due to some foolish choice you made?

God places you in a position of authority because He expects the best from you. He is counting on you to make wise decisions that will bless the people, not hurt them. He relies on you to be an example of goodness, integrity, and honor. God entrusts His people to you, that you will keep the promises you made to him and them. You cannot throw away His trust and the faith of your subordinates by being irresponsible, irrational, and prideful. Learn from the mistake of David. Avoid the trickery of the enemy. There will be tough decisions, but don't let them be anything like the one David had to make.

## PRAYER

*God, please save me from the wicked plots of the enemy to destroy this business You've given me. Let me see his plans before they are made and avoid them. I don't want to be the type of leader that causes death and pain in the lives of my followers. They trust me and so do You. Help me to live up to Your expectations. There will be tough decisions I have to make. Give me the wisdom and knowledge to lead Your people in the right direction. In Jesus' name. Amen.*

# CONFIRMATION

Reading: Jeremiah 32

While Jeremiah was in prison, he said, "The Lord spoke this word to me: Your cousin Hanamel, son of your uncle Sahllum, will come to you soon. Hanamel will say to you, 'Jeremiah, you are my nearest relative, so buy my field near the town of Anathoth. It is your right and duty to buy that field.' Then it happened just as the Lord had said. My cousin Hanamel came to me in the courtyard of the guard and said to me, 'Buy for yourself my field near Anathoth in the land of Benjamin. It is your right and duty to buy it and own it.' So I knew this was a message from the Lord."
**Jeremiah 32:6-8 (NCV)**

God speaks a thing to us then He confirms it. If you ever really want to know if you really heard what you thought you heard from God, ask Him to confirm it. In the book of Jeremiah, the writer recalls hearing the Lord tell him that it was for him to purchase a certain piece of land. He was told that his cousin would come to him, offering the land to him. Later, his cousin actually requests that he buy the land, just as it had been prophesied to him by God. Because of this, he becomes sure that it was for him to buy the property.

When God led me to enter into my first lease on office space, I was really nervous and unsure. Everything in my spirit told me to move forward in faith, but my bank account was singing a completely different tune. I didn't know how I was going to pay the deposit or furnish it, and not being able to pay the monthly rent was a thought I didn't even want to entertain. But the voice of God instructed me to have faith and move forward, so I did. God led me to a property owner who worked with me and gave me a great deal. Eight months passed before I experienced my first battle with coming up with rent money. Twenty-three days after I opened my office doors, I received a design job for an entire house. In the design field, it is common to get partial residential jobs, but full home assignments are rare and complete blessings. My experience with my landlord and the obtaining of a big and much needed job confirmed my movement into my office space and washed away my concerns about paying the monthly rent.

God will speak instructions to you for the purposes of your business. He will then confirm His word through the restlessness of your spirit and the experiences that follow. Never be afraid to ask God to confirm His instructions to you. However, once He does you must move forward in faith. What an insult to God to give his directions twice and then be given a response of disobedience.

## PRAYER

*Father, You speak a thing and then You confirm it. No words that come from Your mouth return to You void. Speak into my life and the life of my business. Give me attentive ears that I will hear every word that is spoken to me. Confirm the things You say to me so that I can move forward in confidence and faith. I trust You that You will not lead me into any situation that You cannot handle or work out for my good. I reverence You, and ask You these things in Jesus' name. Amen.*

# STARTING AGAIN

Reading: Lamentations 3

**The Lord's love never ends; his mercies never stop. They are new every morning; Lord, your loyalty is great. I say to myself, "The Lord is mine, so I hope in him."**
**Lamentations 3:22-24 (NCV)**

Even if we messed up yesterday, today is a new day with new mercies. We are unfaithful, but the Lord is always loyal. Because He knows us better than we know ourselves, He extends to us a new day and a new opportunity to get it right.

Sometimes we beat ourselves up because of the mistakes we've made in the past. Bad choices we made, time we let pass, sins we let overtake us. The good thing is that God does not treat us the way we treat ourselves. He is willing to forget all of our mistakes and separate them from us as far as the east is from the west (Psalm 103:12).

Maybe God told you to open this business five or ten years ago. Possibly, last year you didn't move out in faith and make certain advances in your business that you were supposed to due to fear. Perhaps you ignored the call completely and did your own thing. In spite of your disobedience, God is still standing with wide open arms, welcoming you today to make the right choice.

Aren't you glad we have such a merciful God? Jeremiah, the author of Lamentations was so relieved about the Father's mercy that he says, "The Lord is mine, so I hope in him." Knowing how faithful God is made Jeremiah want to wait on and trust in God. Knowing this should ignite the same feelings within us.

So now that you have been given a new day and another chance to do what is right, what will you do? Will you take advantage of the Lord's mercy and set out to accomplish all that has been requested of you? Will you thank God for a second chance and getting moving? Will you forget your past and look towards a bright future? Or, will you waste another day being unfaithful and foolish? Will you assume you have another day and disregard the call of the Lord? Will you hold onto the things of your past and let them keep you chained to the old you?

Today, when you awoke, the Lord presented you with grace and mercy to start anew. Yesterday is a distant memory and tomorrow is not promised. So praise God for His mercy and faithfulness. Make up your mind to start again, today.

## PRAYER

*Thank You, my Savior, for Your faithfulness to me. Without Your grace and mercy, I would be lost. You didn't have to give me another chance, but You did. I let go of my past because You already have. I choose today to start again. I will not waste another day in disobedience and regret. Tomorrow is not promised so I take time today to fulfill the requests You've made of me. I offer You all of me, Lord. Have Your way. In the name of Jesus Christ. Amen.*

# "GET UP AND GO!"

Reading: Jonah 1

**The Lord spoke his word to Jonah son of Amittai: "Get up, go to the great city of Ninevah, and preach against it, because I see the evil things they do." But Jonah got up to run away from the lord by going to Tarshish. He went to the city of Joppa, where he found a ship that was going to the city of Tarshish. Jonah paid for the trip and went aboard, planning to go to Tarshish to run away from the Lord.**
**Jonah 1:1-3 (NCV)**

The story of Jonah and the whale is another popular and often told biblical narrative. God tells Jonah to go to Ninevah and preach because the people are living sinfully, but Jonah–out of disobedience–gets on a boat, attempting to run away from God. Of course, you can't run from God. Because of his disobedience, God sends a storm and Jonah is thrown overboard. He ends up in the belly of a large fish until he repents and agrees to do what the Lord told him to do initially. Jonah had to go through a whole bunch of drama just because he wouldn't get up and go like God told him to do. Hard-headed.

Many of us are just like Jonah. God is telling us, "Get up and go," but we try to run and hide from the commands of the Lord. Is there something God has told you to do, but you've done everything but that thing? We talk ourselves out of doing God's instructions. We make excuses for why it is not the time to do it or why something else is more important. Truthfully, what is more important than being obedient to God?

When God sends a mission our way there are factors that we don't know concerning why He is selecting us. God knew

Jonah was the right man for the job. He knew Jonah could preach against the city with the passion and conviction that was required to change their ways. When we don't follow the commands of the Lord, we undermine His plans and wisdom.

God has given you vision and instructions for your business for a reason. You may not understand it all, but you have to trust Him regardless. You may not even want to open a business or get involved in a certain industry, but He is moving you to do so. His thoughts and ways are above yours. What you desire to do is not always what is best for you or for others. The reason you may be going through turmoil is because you are on the boat to Tarshish when God told you to go to Ninevah. Do what He has commanded and watch your circumstances turn for the better.

Is God saying to you today, "Get up and go?" Don't worry about the details or what else you think you should be doing, just go. Be willing to move when God says so.

## PRAYER

*Father, forgive me for thinking that I know better than You. There are commands You've given me that I have not been faithful to. Instead of being obedient to You, I ran and hid. Today, I turn away from my Tarshish and go toward my Ninevah. I trust You as you give me instructions concerning my business, even those I don't understand. Be with me in my journey and help me to complete the mission that You have sent me to do. In the name of Jesus. Amen.*

# CHOSEN

Reading: Acts 9

**But the Lord said to Ananias, "Go! I have chosen Saul for an important work. He must tell about me to those who are not Jews, to kings, and to the people of Israel. I will show him how much he must suffer for my name."**

**Acts 9:15-16 (NCV)**

Saul (or better known as Paul) was chosen by God to be an influential participant in early Christianity. Although he originally persecuted the followers of Christ, his purpose was to become one of Christ's most dedicated fans. When you are chosen to do a thing, you don't find it, it finds you.

What calling has found you? What purpose has sought you out and stopped you dead in your tracks? Before I opened my interior design business, I worked full-time in the mental health field as a counselor/therapist for seven years. I knew I no longer wanted to focus my career in psychology anymore, but was preparing to move into the field of education. Someone suggested I would be a great interior decorator and a former passion within me came back to life. Within four months of that suggestion, I had begun taking a design course, created business cards, obtained a business license, and moved into an office. I never intended to do any of it. To be honest, I really didn't want to start a business, but doors kept opening and the Spirit kept pushing me deeper and deeper into this new profession. After a while I came to accept that I had been chosen to start and run a company.

Anytime you are chosen to fulfill a role, it is always about everyone else, but you. For Saul, he was selected to tell the Jews and gentiles about the Lord. The Jews needed leadership and Saul was chosen to help them serve God. However, God also needed a "bad boy" to reach the gentiles. Saul, having come from a different background, could relate to non-Jews. He could communicate to them in ways in which typical Jews were unable. Saul's calling was about God reaching the people who truly needed him. Even in my own life, I've learned that my business is not about me. God gave me a company so that I can give others the opportunities they need. I've grown to desire the development of those underneath me and want to cultivate the passion inside them. My business is also about helping others through the sharing of my learned knowledge and wisdom.

So what have you been chosen to do? How does your business reflect the calling on your life? Is your company still all about you, or have you yielded it to a higher purpose or to the needs of others? Don't hesitate when your calling seeks you out. Accept it, embrace it, and move into it. Realize that God wants to use you through it for the benefit of others. Enjoy being a chosen vessel, poured out by the Almighty.

## PRAYER

*Almighty God, thank You for choosing me. There are so many others in this world You could have selected to use, but You picked me. You believe in me and trust me to positively influence Your people. I accept and embrace this purpose You have brought into my life. I leave my own selfish ambitions behind and yield myself completely to what You would have me to do and the people You would have me to serve. Fill me, Lord, pour me out, and fill me again. In Christ's name. Amen.*

# MUCH, MUCH MORE

Reading: Ephesians 3

**With God's power working in us, God can do much, much more than anything we can ask or imagine.**
**Ephesians 3:20 (NCV)**

By ourselves, we are nothing. Our strength, power, even intelligence is limited and unimpressive. However, when God is added to our lives, we become mountain movers, bondage breakers, and beings who can do much, much more.

"With God's power working in us..." We need the Lord in order to complete every desire of our heart. From waking in the morning, to sleeping at night, even breathing requires the power of God within us. As He moves in our bodies and souls, He fills us with the power that is needed to do the impossible. Because of His presence alone, we are destined for victory.

"...God can do much, much more..." Not just much more, but much, much more. That means He is able to do more than just a lot more. He is capable of doing beyond what is considered a large amount or extent more in our lives.

"...than anything we can ask or imagine." Wow! I have a massive imagination. I love to daydream and always think bigger than most people around me. I never want mediocre; I always want the very best and the most high. But God can do beyond the grandest, most creative, most extensive thoughts and imaginations that I have. Think about how much that means He can do!

As an entrepreneur, this verse should get you excited. A shiver should roll down your spine; goose bumps should appear on your back, arms, and chest. You are just asking for a small business with three or four employees and health insurance. He can top that! You ask for an international, multi-site corporation at the top of the Fortune 500 list. He can beat that too! Whatever you dream up, He can do much, much more!

Stop worrying about the success of your company and start living in it. His power is working in you right now and He is able to do above all that you could ever fathom in your mind. If you could really grasp this concept, you would stop thinking so small and carnally-minded. You would start asking and wishing, and dreaming, and imagining some crazy and outlandish things for your business because you would believe He could do it plus some more. I can't speak for you, but from now on, I am asking for the sun, moon, stars and everything in between!

## PRAYER

*Glorious Lord, how excellent is Your name in all the earth! I am so grateful to have a God in my life that can do great and awesome things that I can't even imagine. Let Your power work in me every day. I know that this business not only will be successful, but it will be blessed and highly favored. I expect You to do much, much more in this business. Surpass my wildest dreams, Lord and give me a testimony that will outdo any worldly coincidence or luck. In the name of Jesus, I ask these blessings. Amen.*

# ENCOURAGE YOURSELF

## Psalm 42

**I say to God, my Rock, "Why have you forgotten me? Why am I sad and troubled by my enemies?" My enemies' insults make me feel as if my bones were broken. They are always saying "Where is your God?" Why am I so sad? Why am I so upset? I should put my hope in God and keep praising him, my Savior and my God.**
**Psalm 42:9-11 (NCV)**

David was a man deeply loved and favored by God, but even David experienced difficult times. David knew what depression and disappointment felt like. There were times when it seemed like his enemies would overtake him. There were times when he felt like God had abandoned him.

Yet even in the lowest of times, when no one around him could offer a word to motivate and uplift him, he knew that God was the answer to his problems. No matter what the situation looked like, he had previously witnessed the unsurpassed power of the Lord and could not deny that God could change his circumstances. In his saddest moments he didn't look to the comfort of others, he simply encouraged himself.

He asks himself an important question. "Why am I so sad?" He knows the power of the Lord, but he still finds himself struggling with his faith. Then he concludes, "I should put my hope in God and keep praising him." David understands that his victory is related to his belief in God and what the Lord can do in his life.

Sometimes you have to encourage yourself. Sometimes there is no one around that can give you a pep talk. Sometimes others around you don't understand what you are going through and therefore can't give you the support you need. In times like these, you will have to do the job yourself. You will have to reach back to all of the memories you have of God rescuing you and apply them to your current situation. You will have to remember how great the Lord is and trust Him despite what you are going through. And you will have to praise Him for the victory, even before it comes.

Being an entrepreneur is, at times, a lonely battle. There will not always be others to fight with and for you. As the leader, you will have to be strong for those under your leadership. You probably will not be able to lean on your subordinates for the support you desire.

David understood the power of encouraging himself. He knew that he could not wait around for anyone else to do it. Stop looking around to your pastor, friends, family, or whomever else to cheer you on and do it for yourself. Read your word, listen to gospel music, pray, write a list of all the spectacular things God has already done for you. Do whatever it takes to motivate, inspire, and encourage yourself.

## PRAYER

*Father God, I come to You in the hardest moments of my life. My situation is gloomy. Depression and fear threaten to take over my spirit. I need You right now to be my strength and my shield. I remember all the wonderful things You have done for me and how You've saved me in the past. I praise You now because I know You are with me and once again, You will deliver me. In You, Lord, I have the victory. In Jesus' name. Amen.*

# DON'T BE FOOLISH

Reading: Judges 16

Then Delilah said to him, "How can you say, 'I love you,' when you don't even trust me? This is the third time you have made a fool of me. You haven't told me the secret of your great strength." She kept bothering Samson about his secret day after day until he felt he was going to die! So he told her everything. He said, "I have never had my hair cut, because I have been set apart to God as a Nazirite since I was born. If someone shaved my head, I would lose my strength and be as weak as any other man."
- Judges 16:15-17 (NCV)

Samson was amazingly strong, but his story demonstrates that even the most powerful people can be brought down by being foolish. Samson was a problem for the Philistines because he could not be captured and was a threat to their lives. His strength was in his hair, but the Philistines would have never known this if it were not for him falling in love with a woman named Delilah–divulging to her his secret. The interesting thing is that it seemed obvious that she was out to trick him because she tried three times to get the truth out of him. He would tell her a lie about where his strength came from then she would try to weaken him by doing what was told to her. When it didn't work, she became upset and asked him again to tell her the secret. Even then, she wouldn't let it go. She nagged him about it until he finally surrendered the truth. Now knowing the truth, she cut his hair which caused him to lose his strength, and turned him over to the Philistines.

The reality is that we all are guilty of having a Samson moment in our lives. All of us have allowed someone or something to weaken us. We have all been foolish when the truth was staring us in the face.

Are there any Delilahs in your life? Is there someone trying to get close to you just to bring you down? Who is that person who every time they come around, you seem to get weak? Alternatively, is there something in your life that holds you back, keeps you bound, or drains your energy? Whoever (or whatever) your Delilah is, you will have to walk away from them (or it) if you really want to enjoy success in your life.

Don't be foolish. If someone is slowing you down or coming against the good you are trying to do, why would you continue to allow it? Most people are obvious about their intentions. If you think a particular person may be bad for you, ask a few of your most trusted friends and family members what they think about that person. If everyone agrees the person is shady, believe them.

You will encounter Delilahs as you pursue building your company. You will become a threat to others and their response will be to attempt to trick you into disclosing your secrets to them. They will plot to expose your weaknesses and ruin you. Your best defenses are to be cautious in the selection of acquaintances and to believe people when they show you their true colors. Don't be foolish. Your business and future is at stake.

## PRAYER

*Jehovah, You are the God of all things. Thank You for the strength You've given me to accomplish my purpose. Give me the wisdom to know who and what are not good for me. Show me if someone or something seeks to drain my strength and block my goals. And Lord, if there are Delilahs in my life, help to me remove these things and people from my path so that I can continue down the road to success. In the name of Jesus. Amen.*

# ASK FOR DISCERNMENT

Reading: John 6

**Then Jesus answered, "I chose all twelve of you, but one of you is a devil. Jesus was talking about Judas, the son of Simon Iscariot. Judas was one of the twelve, but later he was going to turn against Jesus.**
**John 6:70-71 (NCV)**

Jesus was not naïve. He knew one of his disciples would turn on Him and even told them it would happen in advance. Jesus had the gift of discernment. He was able to know who was for Him and who was not.

As business owners, we need the gift of discernment. It is critical to know if those who surround us really care about us or if they are only out to destroy us. Having the ability to discern the hearts of people could be the deciding factor to whether or not your business survives.

What is discernment? Discernment is that nagging feeling you get in the pit of your stomach that cannot be ignored. It's that whisper that keeps telling you, "Be careful!" Even when you want to pass it off as just being paranoid, it continues to haunt you until you finally accept the truth it brings.

The more you learn how to discern people and things, the easier it will be to avoid trouble. You will come to understand that God can protect you from danger by using internal instincts. After a while, you will discover how the gift works and you'll stop questioning the Spirit when it reveals various motivations to you.

How do you receive the gift of discernment? Ask God for it. The Lord promises to withhold no good thing from us. Jesus tells us that if we ask for anything in the name of Jesus, He would give it to us so that the Father could be gloried through the Son. The bible reminds us to ask God for wisdom and assures us that He will free give it to us.

If you need the Lord to lead you and guide you in your relationships and associations, ask Him for discernment. If you want to make good decisions regarding who your true friends are and who has hidden agendas, ask for discernment. If you want to avoid trickery and deceit, ask God for the spirit of discernment.

In Proverbs 3:5, the word tells us that if we acknowledge God in everything that we do, he will give us direction. Discernment is a form of direction. Be wise and seek God every day for every choice you must make. Ask Him for the gift of discernment today.

## PRAYER

*Almighty Lord, thank you for all of the good things You have given to me. Thank You for this business and the many blessing you have prepared for it. I ask that You help me to maintain it by giving me the Spirit of Discernment. I want to make the right choices about people and things that are around me, but I cannot do it unless I know the truth about them. Bestow unto me discernment so that I will know who loves me and who hates me. Keep me from falling naively into the traps of evil. Jesus, You know how it feels to be betrayed. Thank You God for this gift You offer me today. In Jesus' name. Amen.*

# A GOOD REPUTATION

Reading: Proverbs 22: 1-16

**A good name is more desirable than great riches; to be esteemed is better than silver and gold.**
**Proverbs 22:1 (NIV)**

A bad reputation is a sure way to destroy your company. Especially if you are in your beginning stages or considered a small business, the last thing want to do is create a bad name for yourself. Businesses require customers, vendors, and employees, but no one wants to be involved with a company that is known for doing unprofessional, dishonest, or unreliable business.

There are many ways to earn a good reputation and creating one begins with the love of God. If you truly love God and seek Him every day and in every way, your thoughts and actions will always led to good decisions that promote a good reputation. Have you ever met someone that was so full of God's love that they wouldn't hurt a fly and could be trusted in every way? The light inside them radiates onto all they come into contact with and forces others to assess their own righteousness. That is the kind of person we should be striving to be. With a light so bright, a good reputation is inevitable.

On the flip side, building a bad reputation is actually very easy to do. Just abandon all the principles of God and conduct business using the world's and Satan's methods. Lie, cheat, steal, manipulate, be inconsistent, selfish, unreliable, lazy, untrustworthy, tactless, unprofessional–must I go on? It may sound silly that I am even discussing this issue, but believe me, have seen many "Christians" operating their business in very ungodly ways.

I once was told a story about an interior designer who was given a large lump sum of money by a client and after six months did not provide any services for the client's home. In addition, the designer refused to produce receipts for all the purchases the designer claimed to have made for the client. When I heard the story, I thought to myself, "This person really doesn't want to keep their business. They are begging for a lawsuit and destroying their reputation!" I'm pretty sure the person did not intend to place himself or herself in such a bad predicament, but most likely due to abandoning the principles of God's word this person dug a hole deep enough to bury themselves and their business in it.

A good name will keep your business surviving when others are fading away. With all the loss of integrity in the business world it is invaluable to be known as one who does what is right. Ask God to protect your name and your business' reputation from anything that seeks to destroy it.

## PRAYER

*Almighty God, fill me with Your love and let it overflow from my life onto all others that I meet. I desire to create and maintain a good reputation. I do not want to destroy my business by doing destructive and unwise things. Place Your principles so deep in my heart that without thinking, I abide by them. Protect my name from the enemy and his attempts to ruin the vision You've given to me. In the name of Jesus. Amen.*

# GOOD ADVICE

Reading: Proverbs: 15

**Plans fail without good advice, but they succeed with the advice of many others. People enjoy giving good advice. Saying the right word at the right time is so pleasing.**

**Proverbs 15: 22-23 (NCV)**

Reality check: you don't know everything. I know it's hard to accept, but the quicker you do, the better off you'll be. There is always more to know. Even the most brilliant scholars spend numerous hours doing research because they've learned that there is more information out there to be acquired.

Another fascinating detail about life is that people have unique experiences and differing perspectives. Depending on what an individual has been through, their experiences will alter their world schema. This means that as you share knowledge with others, you not only have the chance to give wisdom directly related to your experiences, but you also can obtain insight based on the experiences of others. Both people have the opportunity to walk away with a greater understanding for things in this life.

It is wonderful to receive good advice, and even better to give it. Writing this book, I am enjoying being able to pass down some of the hard lessons I have learned as I've experienced entrepreneurship. I also have appreciated the wisdom that others who also have started businesses have spoken to me. One of my most memorable experiences of receiving good advice about business ownership came from talking with a lawyer. I needed a lawyer for my business to help me with creating legal documents and giving me legal advice as needed. I stumbled upon the business card of a man who working in the same office complex as me who offered these services. When I met with him for the first time, I was skeptical about him because of the reputation lawyers usually get for being corrupt and narcissistic people. To my surprise, he was everything but this. His guidance and suggestions during our brief meeting empowered me to not be afraid to take more control over my business and learn more for myself. I walked away feeling liberated and inspired, with no doubts that he should become my business' attorney.

Receiving good advice is a treasure. Not everyone can give you the right word at the right time. When you hear something that you really need to hear, your spirit praises God for the on-time wisdom. Giving good advice is also a gift. It demonstrates that you have taken something positive from your experiences–even the worst ones. If you've learned to grow in this way, not only will you be in a position to give good advice, but you will also be able to live according to the good advice you have received.

## PRAYER

*Thank you God for the good advice you give to me daily through Your word, though the Holy Spirit, and through others. Surround me with people who can counsel me and give me the good advice I need to make good business decisions. Also, as I learn through my experiences, help me not to be selfish, but to be willing to give good advice to others who need it. I praise You for always knowing what I need to hear and when I need to hear it. I also glorify You for using me as a vessel to speak wisely to those You send my way. In Jesus' name Amen.*

# MY BUSINESS, HIS WAY

Reading: Ephesians 4

**Those who are stealing must stop stealing and start working. They should earn an honest living for themselves. Then they will have something to share with those who are poor.**

**Ephesians 4:28 (NCV)**

God allows you to be an entrepreneur for two reasons, to help you earn an honest living and to provide you with a means to help others. Now that you have moved into business ownership, there is no cause for you to do illegal, inappropriate, or ungodly things to make money. You might not have the surplus you desire, but you should have at least enough to take care of your basic needs.

Your company not only opens doors for you, but it also can be used as a vehicle for assistance to others. As you develop your company, remind yourself of the dual role your business plays. Your business decisions should reflect a desire to take care of yourself and your family as well as help others. Ask yourself these questions: How does your business help you? Does it provide for your family so that you don't have to steal to meet you basic needs? How does your company help others? Do you offer jobs to the community? Do you give to charitable causes? Do you offer pro bono services or free products to the poor? Does your business uplift and promote the Kingdom of Heaven?

If your business is all about you and only benefits you, then it is not operating according to the word of God. Owning a company that is endorsed by the Lord is about doing things His way. Yes, the business is in your name, but He is the foundation of your company and insists that you manage your business in a way that reflects the Christ in you. Running your business any other way just won't do.

Let go of every thought and notion that exalts itself against the knowledge of God (2 Corinthians 10:5). Your business should be an extension of the body of Christ. The only way you can expect the vision to come to past is to conduct business His way. God's way is reaching out to the poor and the lost. When Jesus was on earth, He didn't stay to Himself or surround Himself only by the rich and prominent. He made Himself available to the people who needed His touch, His love, His mercy, and His truth. We must demonstrate these same principals in our lives through our businesses. Every day you walk through the front door of your office, answer your business phone line, or head out to service another customer, mediate on this: I will operate my business, His way.

## PRAYER

*Thank you, Father that I don't have to steal to meet my needs and those of my family. I am working and earning an honest living through this business You have blessed me with. Let my company not only benefit me, but let it also help others. I want to be able to give back, just as freely as You've given to me. Let this company reflect all that is good. God, I give You complete control to lead me in the direction that you feel my business should go. This is my business, but You are free to have Your way through it. In the name of Jesus Christ. Amen.*

# IT'S YOUR TIME

Reading: Isaiah 54

**The Lord says, "Sing, Jerusalem. You are like a woman who never gave birth to children. Start singing and shout for joy. You never felt the pain of giving birth, but you will have more children than the woman who has a husband. Make your tent bigger; stretch it out and make it wider. Do not hold back. Make the ropes longer and its stakes stronger, because you will spread out to the right and to the left. Your children will take over other nations, and they will again live in cities that once were destroyed.**
**Isaiah 54:1-3 (NCV)**

A common cliché is used when someone wants something and after a long period of waiting, still has not received it. "It's just not your time." A woman with children will tell a barren woman, "It's not your time." A married woman will tell a single woman, "It's not your time." These words can be the most difficult to hear and accept, especially when the person telling you this already has what you want.

However, what happens when your time finally comes? If it wasn't your time in the past, eventually your time must come. Isaiah prophesied to Jerusalem telling them their time had come. No more waiting around in misery and sadness. No more watching others obtain the blessings you've been craving. No more tears, no more struggles. How wonderful is it when your turn comes and your time is now?

God is preparing you for something big. The only way you can receive it is if you're ready. So in anticipation for his blessing he is saying, "Stretch out, make more room, get ready." You have to make room for what God wants to do in your life. If you don't enlarge your territory, you won't be able to contain what he wants to do. For example, if you lived in a one-bedroom apartment and already had your place fully furnished, then I come along and give you three bedrooms full of furniture, where are you going to keep it all? You can't wait until the day I bring the moving truck full of furniture to your front door before your begin making arrangements, you have to prepare yourself in advance. It may mean throwing out your outdated stuff, getting a storage unit, or upgrading to a bigger apartment or house. Whatever you decide to do, these choices and plans must be made prior to the delivery date. The same thing works with the blessings of the Lord. If God is telling you he wants to increase your business, you have to make room for the expansion. You may have to get a bigger office, hire more people, advertise on a larger scale, or get rid of some "old things" that will not be necessary when God pulls up with the delivery truck full of new blessings. These "old things" could include old relationships, pain, baggage, resources, ways, and tangible objects that are worn out and defeat the purpose.

Your time is coming. That is not the question. The question is will you be ready when it comes? If you are not, the delivery truck may pull off with your blessings still inside. So right now, in advance, make room. Enlarge your tents, make your ropes long, make your stakes stronger, and don't hold back.

## PRAYER

*I hear Your voice, Lord, telling me to make room. I believe that You will transform me from being barren to being the producer of many. In faith, I prepare for Your blessings by enlarging my territory. I don't want You to show up with all that You have for me and I am not ready. I believe that my time for business success is soon and coming. I wait patiently and expectantly for You, Great God. In Christ Jesus' name. Amen.*

# ALL TALK

Reading: Proverbs 14

**Those who work hard make a profit, but those who only talk will be poor.**
**Proverbs 14:23 (NCV)**

Have you ever met someone who was all talk? Someone who is always going on and on about what they have, what they use to have, and what they are going to have? Someone who always has a new plan or idea, but rarely follows through on anything they say? Someone who has a million dreams, yet hasn't even taken the first step towards even one of them?

Maybe you are that person. You keep saying you are going back to school or going to open your business, but you haven't even picked up an application to any schools or created business cards yet. You constantly reminisce on what you "used" to have and how good life "used" to be. You brag about how talented you are and how much potential you have, but you won't take any initiative towards using your abilities to uplift yourself or anyone else.

*Those who work hard make a profit.* As the old folks say, "Money doesn't grow on trees." If you want to obtain financial rewards, you will have work hard to earn them. Your dreams won't happen on their own, you have to bring them to life through commitment, sacrifice, and sweat. Starting and running a business is not an easy task. Your all will be required from day one and monetary benefits probably will not appear instantly. Entrepreneurship involves working harder now for yourself than you ever had to work for someone else. You do it to make a profit. Profits come in different forms: monetary, self-fulfillment, helping others, benefits to society, and growth and development.

*But those who only talk will be poor.* Working hard earns you a profit, but talk earns you nothing. Talkers remain uneducated, unemployed, and unfulfilled. Talkers stay broke because they don't make the moves needed to make money. Talkers miss out on all of the various types of profit due to their unproductive lip service.

To be a successful business owner you must be a hard worker. Talking alone will not get you to the Promised Land. Every day ask yourself, "What can I do today to move one step closer to my goals?" Don't tell anyone your goals if you have no intention of achieving them, it only makes you look foolish. Decide today that you will be more than a poor talker; you will be a profitable, hard worker.

## PRAYER

*Almighty God, who gives us the ability to obtain wealth. I thank You for blessing me with all the gifts, talents, and skills You've instilled within me. I praise You for the business ideas and plans You've spoken over my life. I ask that You help me to be a doer and not just a talker. I know that all talk leads to poverty and that is not where I want to be. Give me the strength, the courage, and the power every day to work hard and move in the direction of my goals. Overflow my life with all of the profits of hard work. I ask this in the name of Jesus. Amen.*

# WATCH WHAT YOU SAY

Reading: Proverbs 13 & 15

**Those who are careful about what they say protect their lives, but whoever speaks without thinking will be ruined.**
**Proverbs 13:3 (NCV)**

**A gentle answer will calm a person's anger, but an unkind answer will cause more anger.**
**Proverbs 15:1 (NCV)**

You've invested your money, time, and heart into your business. Although you may be an extremely professional person, there will be times when you will be tempted to respond to others in ways that could hurt you and your business. Too much is at risk to speak without thinking so you must be careful and watch what you say.

It is so easy to speak without thinking. There are many thoughts and beliefs that we all have that should be kept private or only disclosed to people in our inner circles. It is not that you don't have a right to your opinion, but speaking the wrong thing in the wrong environment could be inappropriate and very damaging. You now have more to consider than just yourself, you also must consider your business.

"A fool's mouth is his destruction" Proverbs 18:7 (NCV). Avoid destroying your company with words that come from your mouth. The enemy is lurking, waiting for you to give him the opportunity to rip apart what God has blessed you with. You give him the ammunition he needs when you speak hastily.

Even as you deal with customers and employees, remember to restrain your tongue. Indeed, some people deserve a good tongue-lashing, but will that solve the problem or promote your company? Probably not. You can communicate the same ideas using a professional and gentle tone. Both what you say and how you say it will impact how it is received by the person you are communicating with.

You have a responsibility to care for your business which includes presenting yourself at all times as a role model, leader, and Christian. People are not as forgiving as the Lord is and will hold what you say against you. One inappropriate comment could be the death of your beloved business. Is it really worth it? Do you want your mouth to be your destruction? Do you want to cause more anger and strife through unkind and rash words? Protect yourself, your peace, and your company. Watch what you say.

## PRAYER

*Lord, there are so many times when I find myself saying or tempted to say things that could potentially hurt my business and my reputation. I don't want to be the fool who ruins his life and destroys himself with his own mouth. Help me to tame my tongue. Show me when it is inappropriate to say certain things. Reveal to me whom I can speak to frankly, and whom I cannot. Let my words to others be gentle and professional at all times. Protect me from the traps of the enemy to speak out of anger and hast. In Jesus' name, I pray. Amen.*

# REDEFINING SUCCESS

Reading: Proverbs 13

**Some people pretend to be rich but really have nothing. Others pretend to be poor but really are wealthy.**

**Proverbs 13:7 (NCV)**

There are people who live in mansion-style homes, drive the finest cars, dine at the most expensive restaurants, wear the best clothing, rock the most glamorous jewelry, and hang with only the elite. From the outside, it seems as if the world is theirs. Struggle and hard times seem to not know their address. The world envies them, wishing for just a taste of their lives. Yet with all they have, everything that matters most eludes them.

Then there are others who live with next-to-nothing. They may ride the bus or drive an outdated car, eat bologna sandwiches and drink store brand soda, live in a studio or one bedroom apartment, wear thrift store clothing and plastic jewelry, and befriend people just as penniless as themselves. The rich look down at them and pity them for their material-less lives, glad a better hand was dealt to them. But with the little the poor have, life's most precious gifts are abundant to them.

Success is not about how much money you have or don't have. Success is not about education, career, or social status. Society tells us that this is the definition of success, but in reality, it is not. Success is relevant. We each have the ability to define what success is for ourselves. One person may view being successful as owning their own small business; another requires a Fortune 500 label to feel the same.

Success is what you decide in your mind is necessary for you to feel that you've achieved what you set out to do. Some people will never be successful because they haven't set goals for themselves or because they've let others do the honors. You could have all the money in the world, but money can't fill your heart or soul.

Alternatively, many people who appear monetarily successful are frauds. They can't be happy or enjoy any of their materialistic gain because they are stressed-out from the bills associated with all they have, needing to work nonstop to maintain it all. That is definitely not a healthy definition of success.

For the person who always wanted to be a teacher and now instructs a third grade class, that person knows success. For the person who just wanted to sing and now is a background singer for a major artist, that person knows success. And for you who wanted to start a business–whether it be a salon, computer repair shop, record store, grocery store, temp agency, clothing store, law office, medical center, advertising agency, counseling center, nonprofit organization, or design studio–and are now doing just that, you know success. Redefine success to meet your own standards. Don't worry about what the world wants you to be or thinks about you. If you earn a billion dollars or only a few hundred, you still are a success story.

## PRAYER

*My God, I thank You that I don't have to live up to others' expectations. Today I choose to define success for myself. The dreams You've put inside of me determines the level of my achievements. I don't have to make millions of dollars or drive a fancy car to be important. I am proud of the business I have created and will enjoy the fruits of my success. My life reflects that of a person who set out to do something great and achieved it. Thank You, Father. In Jesus' name. Amen.*

# KNOW WHO YOU ARE

Reading: Mark 15

**Pilate asked Jesus, "Are you the king of the Jews?" Jesus answered, "Those are your words." The leading priest accused Jesus of many things. So Pilate asked Jesus another question, "You can see that they are accusing you of many things. Aren't you going to answer?" But Jesus still said nothing, so Pilate was very surprised.**

**Mark 15:2-5 (NCV)**

If you do not define yourself, others will attempt to define you. They will make their assumptions about you then try to mold you into what they want you to be. If you are not clear about who you are, you will eventually find yourself changing to suit the needs of others. One day you may even look in the mirror and not recognize the person looking back at you.

When Jesus was on trial, they tried to define Him by rumors they had heard about Him. They wanted to provoke Him into saying the wrong thing so that they could have a reason to kill Him. However, Jesus knew who He was and decided not to answer their silly questions. He didn't have to prove himself to them by arguing about His title or name.

Once you really know who you are, what others think will become unimportant to you. You won't care if someone likes you or if they don't. You won't be concerned about fitting in with a certain crowd or obtaining the approval of a particular group. You won't even care if someone mispronounces your name or says something fictitious about you. Many of us get caught up in pleasing people. We become totally stressed out over what somebody said or heard. You are a business owner now. A leader cannot be entangled in a bunch of chaos and commotion. There are too many other imperative things to consume your mind and time with rather than the games that non-ambitious people play.

Try this practical assignment. Devote 30 days to working on you. In that time reflect upon and assess who you are and who you feel God has made you to be. Ponder your current attitudes and behaviors. Analyze your thoughts. Ask yourself, "Do I feel good about the person I've become or if there is still more work to do for me to be comfortable with myself?" Decide what it will take for you to love yourself and be more confident. Create a plan for how you will trade old counterproductive behaviors for new productive ones. Allow yourself to move towards a better you over one month's time.

You can't lead a company towards greatness if you–the leader–don't embrace your own significance. You have to know who you are and whom you belong to. If you understand that you are blessed because you belong to God, it will be easier to comprehend that your business is also blessed because it belongs to you. Then you can stand up against the world and naysayers like Jesus did and hold your tongue. To them, you don't have to prove a thing.

## PRAYER

*Jesus, just like You, I want to know who I am. The more confident I am about the person You created me to be, the easier it will be to not allow others to transform me into their expectations. I cannot be consumed with unimportant matters and the questioning of my name. I have to remain focused on this business You've given me and fulfilling the mission You've sent me to complete. Reveal to me Your mysteries, so that as I get to know You, I can better understand myself. Let Your light be reflected in me and help me to stand, unconcerned about proving myself to anyone but You. Amen.*

# SURVIVING THE STORM

Reading: Proverbs 10

**A storm will blow the evil person away, but the good person will always be safe.**
**Proverbs 10:25 (NCV)**

I once heard a preacher say, "In life, storms will come. The question is not if they will come, it is when they will come." If you've lived long enough, you know this to be true. Storms are unavoidable. Life cannot always be happy, times cannot always be good. Every storm is unique and brings its own set of problems with it. Last year's storm could have been within your family, last month's storm could've been financial, and tomorrow's storm could be career related.

Your business will also face storms. The rain will beat on the spiritual windows of your company; the wind will hurl and threaten to blow you and your vision away. But Proverbs informs us that when a storm comes, although the evil person may be destroyed, the good person will survive.

The good person outlasts the storm for two reasons. First, because Good is with them. He becomes the strong tower that they can run to and find safety. He upholds them in his hand; He protects them and keeps them hidden underneath His wings (Psalm 61). When you have God on your side, there is nothing that can harm you; nothing and no one that you should fear. He will bring you through the toughest times victoriously. You won't even hit your foot against a rock (Psalm 91).

Second, because there is a blessing in the storm. Only good people realize this. No matter what you experience, strength, faith, and lessons can be obtained during a storm. Storms shape us, purge us, and remove from us the things that are not like God. It is in our valleys where we come face-to-face with God and are confronted about our weaknesses.

If you are good, you will see the other side of the storm. However, when you come out you should be changed. If you are still the same person after the storm, you missed the point and another storm will brew eventually to teach you what you didn't get the first time. God desires to recreate you into the person he imagined when he designed you. Sin has deteriorated you into something lower than your original design, but the Lord can still restore you. Your storms are his attempts to remold you, but instead, you view them as a curse.

Hard times are not painless; nevertheless, if we think positively and trust God, they will be easier to endure. Not only can we survive them, but also we can come out of them with more power and perfection than we had before. As you persevere through your storm, ask yourself, "What lessons am I learning? What is God showing me or teaching me? In what areas am I growing? In what ways am I changing? What are the benefits of this trial?" The Lord is with you and you will survive. But will you make the journey worth it?

# PRAYER

*Righteous One, You are my Protector and my Provider. As I face the inevitable storms of my life and in my business, I need You to defend me. Give me shelter and surround me in Your loving arms. My storms are not in vain so use them to bring me closer to You. Teach me how to be a better me; show me how to be a better entrepreneur. Bring me out better than I came in, stronger, wiser, and more faithful. I pray these things in Your name, Jesus. Amen.*

# FINISH WHAT YOU STARTED

Reading: Ecclesiastes 7

**It is better to finish something than to start it. It is better to be patient than to be proud.**
**Ecclesiastes 7:8 (NCV)**

We learn in Ecclesiastes that finishing is actually better than starting. There is more to gain from completion than from initiation and yes, finishing is worth it. Knowing this truth why don't most of us complete what we started? Answer: the experiences that come between the start and the end keep many of us from being successful. True, it is hard to accomplish some things; however, the second part of this verse gives us the key to finishing: patience.

Finishing this book has been a challenge for me. I've always dreamed of becoming a published author; it's been in my veins since birth. I've begun innumerous stories, ideas, and manuscripts, but somewhere along the way felt they weren't good enough and abandoned them like irreparable, outdated electronics. My dream to write a book never died, but my ability to finish what I started was nonexistent. After many years of unpublished discontent, the Lord once again reminded me of my dream and His gift. I brokenly browsed countless books in bookstores written by everyone but me. I knew that the reason I wasn't as blessed and fulfilled as I should be was because I wasn't being true to me. With all of the various ways I demonstrated my talents, I failed to give the world the one thing that meant the most to me–my written words.

As I prepare to complete this book and send it off for publishing, I can relate to the Wisdom of Solomon. Finishing this book, and watching a long awaited dream come true is truly better than all the years I spent starting manuscripts that may never see the light of day. Completing this endeavor has required patience from me. I had to be willing to wait for the inspiration, wait through the experiences that led to the wisdom in this book, wait through the writing process, and wait as it is being published. However, my waiting is worth it because the end result is realizing a lifelong goal.

Your business is worth waiting for. You may find yourself struggling with the time it takes to achieve certain milestones in your company. You may have to wait for certain licenses, permits, and approvals. You may have to wait on customers, wait to make money, and wait for employees. Genuine success is not obtained overnight. Regardless of the time that it takes, wait on it. Don't give up. Don't turn your back on your dream. Believe the words of Solomon: Finishing is so much better than beginning.

## PRAYER

*Alpha and Omega, You are the beginning and the end. My faith and love is completed in You. I have dreams and goals in this life that I desire to fulfill. Help me to not only be someone that starts, but help me also to be one who finishes. As I continue to build my business, let me not be dismayed by hard times, frustrations, or a delayed harvest. Let patience resound in me as I wait through it all to see the conclusion of the matter. I trust You, Lord and I promise myself not to give up on me. In Jesus' name. Amen.*

# THE END

Reading: Proverbs 19

**Listen to advice and accept instruction, and in the end you will be wise.**
**Proverbs 19:20 (NIV)**

How will your story end? When all is said and done, how will people remember you? What words will be spoken at your eulogy; what mark will you have left in this world? Will God be pleased with you; or will you have severe consequences to face? In everything we do, we must take into consideration the end result.

Proverbs tells us if we are open to advice and instruction we will be wise in the end. Who doesn't want to be wise? If you own a business, gaining wisdom should be a top priority. Someone who is wise is more likely to make a profit than someone who is foolish.

Proverbs 14:1 states, "The wise woman builds her house, but with her own hands the foolish one tears hers down" (NIV). You have the power to either build your business or tear it down. I have watched "should've been great" businesses fall apart due to the misguidance of their leaders. Major mistakes, poor judgment in consulting, trusting the wrong people, dishonesty, fear, doubt, betrayal, greed, and a zillion other bad choices have led to the destruction of "good idea" companies. It feels bad to fail, but it feels worse to know that failure could've been prevented.

Develop your vision through good counsel and reliable instruction. It will take a lot of hard work, determination, resources, and favor from God to make your business thrive. You cannot afford to make senseless errors that threaten your dream.

Keep in mind the big picture. What is it that you want in the end? The only way you will know if you are moving in the right direction is if you know where you started and where you are headed. Seeking, accepting, and internalizing wisdom must occur while you're en route to your destination if success is a part of your plans.

This book is full of advice and instruction from someone who has walked a day in your shoes. If you are willing to open your mind and heart to the insight found in these pages, you will become a wiser, smarter, and better leader. Let the memory of you be one that reminds the world of what faith in God can do. Let your end result be that of wisdom.

## PRAYER

*Alpha and Omega, You know what the end will be. I pray today that You will guide me towards a wise ending. Let everything that I do from this moment on be fruitful, smart, and pleasing to You. When the right advice and instruction comes my way, allow me to embrace it with an open heart. Do not let pride, deceit, or foolishness block my sight or keep me from counsel that is meant to help my business grow. I cannot do this without You, God. You have brought me from such a mighty long way and I truly believe that You will carry me to the end. In the blessed name of Jesus. Amen.*

# CONCLUSION

**"For my thoughts are not your thoughts, neither are your ways my ways," declares the Lord.**
**Isaiah 55:8 (NIV)**

We are living in difficult times. Beginning a business or even trying to maintain one right now can be very frustrating and disappointing. However, if God has planted a seed of entrepreneurship within you and led you into this season, do not be dismayed. His thoughts are not our thoughts and His ways are not our ways.

It has been about a month since I have completed this book. A month ago I thought I had written my last statement for this project, but I was wrong. Something in my spirit kept nudging me to write a little more, a few final words. Over the past month, God has helped me to experience what it is to truly trust him beyond what I can do for myself. He has also taught me not to worry about what I do not understand, but to know He is with me and He is always in control.

I am a perfectionist and an extremely independent person. Owning a business has moved me completely out of my comfort zone and into a place of total dependence on the Lord. On my own, I am not good enough, smart enough, talented enough, or even strong enough. No matter what I do, I will fail because my power is limited and easily crushed under the weight of this world. But God has brought me into this position at this time to humble me, break me, and rebuild me. The reconstruction of A'ndrea has begun, and although I cannot comprehend all of his plans, I see a new me emerging.

Gods knows your pain. He sees your desire to please Him and to fulfill this dream you've set out to accomplish. He is aware of the hardships, setbacks, risks, sacrifices, and tears.

You thought it was going to be easier, but it has turned out to be one of the steepest mountains you've ever climbed. In the midst of the tests and trials that are sure to come, remember this: His thoughts and ways are not yours. You don't have to understand Him, but in order to make it you will have to trust Him. Believe in God despite how bad things may seem. Expect improvement and production regardless of what you hear in the media. Wait on your breakthrough and keep praying no matter how many other businesses fail. Those of us who win in the end will be those that did not recede.

When the enemy attacks you with lies of negativity, cynicism, and pessimism, turn to the supports in your life (prayer, friends, family, Bible, this book, etc.) to keep you focused on God's truth. Things may not work out exactly the way you planned, but they will work out. In my final words to you, I cannot begin to emphasize the importance of continuous, non-stop, never ending faith in God. You are the person the Lord has set apart to run and build this business in this season. You are special and unlike anyone around you. Everything you need to become a success story is either already inside of you or will be given to you in His time. Don't give up because it's hard or because it hurts. Like the popular saying goes, "To have something you never had you must do something you've never done." Trust God with a faith you've never expressed before. Place all that you possess at his feet and believe that He is God. In the end, He will be glorified through your business, His way.

## MY PRAYER FOR YOU

*Almighty God, this book is ending, but Your faithfulness never will. You know all including the road this entrepreneur must walk. You understand every need, every desire, and every emotion that they have even before they experience it. Abide with them, Lord. Let Your presence be felt every step of the way. When they cannot comprehend*

*Your plans, remind them that You are God and You are still in control. As they place their dreams at Your feet, give them the favor and blessing that they require to establish this business You've spoken over their life. Fill them with wisdom and knowledge so that they can be a good steward over their company. When they feel afraid and exhausted, endow them with a triple portion of faith and strength. Without faith it is impossible to please You. I bind, in the name of Jesus, every doubt that attempts to come against their belief. From this moment on they will walk in complete trust in You, no matter what. And because of their faith, You will save, bless, and heal them and their business. In Jesus Christ's name. Amen.*

# Q & A with the Author: 5 Years Later

Five years later, **Dr. A'ndrea J. Wilson** answers commonly asked questions for My Business His Way, Second Edition

Q: What caused you to write My Business His Way?

A: I owned an interior design business in the midst of a failing economy; however, I remained hopeful that God would protect and preserve me despite the world around me. That positive attitude caused others to come to me for encouragement. Eventually, I knew God wanted me to provide others with a written resource of these encouraging thoughts and words.

Q: Do you still own that business? If not, what happened?

A: No, I don't. There was a point when God told me that my business would not continue. It was hard to accept because I didn't understand. Why would God lead me to this venture, have me write about it, and then allow it to fail? But God had another plan for my life and my first business wasn't the end of the story, it was just a part of the process. Once I trusted God enough to let go, He ushered me into a new chapter of my life, freeing me from physical, mental, and emotional weights that were holding me back, and bringing me into my true calling: writing. I now own a different business, a publishing company named Divine Garden Press. My publishing company is so much more likely to succeed in the long run because of the wisdom gained from running the interior design business.

Q: What spiritual advice would you give someone who is considering starting a business now (outside of what is included in this book)?

A: Trust God no matter what. He has a plan for you and if you are willing to submit to His plan, you will see how amazing His plans are for you. There may be rough times and the outcomes may not be what you expected, but continue to rely upon and let your confidence be in Him. He has a way of making everything beautiful in its time.

Q: What business advice would you give someone who is considering starting a business now (outside of what is included in this book)?

A: Control your overhead. One of the things that hurts most businesses, including my first one, was I owed too much to too many people. Don't allow yourself to be burdened by debt and financial obligations. Keep your expenses low, even if that means having to build slowly. You cannot make money if you always have to pay out.

Q: Five years after writing this book, do you think the content is still relevant?

A: Absolutely. The Word of God does not change, neither does God. Even reading through this book again myself, I am amazed at the wisdom within its pages, truth that I must remember now as I lead my current business.

Q: If someone has a business that is failing, would you recommend that they give up or fight to keep it open?

A: I recommend that they seek the guidance of God. Sometimes, it is time to let go, but only God can confirm the end of a venture. Other times, struggle is a part of the journey.

Giving up prematurely is the last thing a business owner should do. Yet even in these cases, only God can direct a person in this manner and give them the strength they need to stand through the trials.

Q: Are you available for speaking engagements related faith and business?

A: Certainly. I can be contacted for booking inquires at drajwilson@gmail.com or via the contact form on my website at www.andreawilsononline.com

Made in the USA
Middletown, DE
19 August 2018